*The Home Book of
Italian Cookery*

By the same author
THE ADVENTUROUS COOK:
RECIPES FROM OUT OF THE WAY PLACES
EATING IN THE OPEN
PRESERVES: HOW TO MAKE AND USE THEM

THE HOME BOOK OF ITALIAN COOKERY

by

Beryl Gould-Marks

FABER AND FABER LIMITED

*First published in 1969
by Faber and Faber Limited
3 Queen Square London WC1
First published in this edition 1974
Printed in Great Britain by
Whitstable Litho, Whitstable, Kent
All rights reserved*

ISBN 0 571 08219 X (hard bound edition)

ISBN 0 571 10590 4 (Faber Paper Covered Edition)

CONDITIONS OF SALE

This book is sold subject to the condition that it shall not, by way of trade or otherwise, be lent, re-sold, hired out or otherwise circulated without the publisher's prior consent in any form of binding or cover other than that in which it is published and without a similar condition including this condition being imposed on the subsequent purchaser

© *Beryl Gould-Marks 1969*

FOR MY HUSBAND AND SON
THE ALWAYS WILLING GUINEA PIGS

Contents

INTRODUCTION	page 11
ITALY FROM NORTH TO SOUTH	15
HERBS	19
SPICES	22
HORS D'OEUVRE	25
ITALIAN PORK PRODUCTS AND SAUSAGES	27
SOUPS	36
PASTA	46
DUMPLINGS	61
RICE	68
PIZZAS	75
EGGS	80
FISH	85
MEAT	98
POULTRY AND GAME	121
VEGETABLES	133
SAUCES	148
DESSERTS	156
CHEESES	172
DRINKS AND APERITIFS	174
LIQUEURS AND SPIRITS	176
INDEX	177

Introduction

Italy, land of history and romance, magically invokes antiquity, sunshine and sea. After the Etruscans had vanished, Roman roads carried the Latin influence far and wide. Just as much as the victorious Romans influenced the eating habits of the peoples they subjugated, so they, in their turn, were influenced. They brought back unheard-of delicacies and ideas from the countries they had conquered.

The Italians have always been imaginative innovators. Long ago they gave ice cream to Europe, and French haute cuisine stemmed from the imported Tuscany chefs of Catherine of Medici. Nowadays Italian cooks and waiters are a major export, and more and more Italian restaurants, trattorias and tavernas are springing up in unexpected places. Pasta, spaghetti, macaroni, ravioli, Parmesan cheese, Marsala, Chianti and scampi are world-famous.

I have been visiting Italy for most of my life, and have learnt to love their food—both urban and country-style—although some of it in small villages can seem fairly primitive.

I first studied Italian cooking during three long trips I made on the same Italian liner. I persuaded the purser to let me explore the galley—if such a vast ship's kitchen can be so called. Here I saw first-class food cooked in quantity. The menus were always more Italian than international.

When my husband was working in Rome, I went to live there. We shared a flat with a delightful scatter-brained woman. Luckily for me, the services of her maid were included. Maria was a charming and efficient Florentine, knowledgeable in regional cooking, too, as she had travelled all over Italy. She taught me Italian home cooking in my own, temporary, kitchen.

I learnt that a pestle and mortar is indispensable. I learnt how to

Introduction

cook pasta asciutta al dente, firm to the tooth as the Italians like it; foamy, Marsala-laced zabaglione and a vast gamut of other dishes. I realized that the unusual texture and flavour of pine nuts (pignoli) can 'make' a dish, either savoury or sweet. These come from the stone pine. I used to pick them up amongst the scented pine needles, or coax them out of their cones. Pine nuts are on sale in many health food stores and specialist shops.

For the first time I appreciated the flavour of fine olive oil, universally used in Italy. There are many different kinds, from the full-flavoured oil of Tuscany to the more delicate one from Abruzzi.

I made full use of their range of cheese. Ricotta, a special curd cheese, is good eaten on its own, or as a filling for ravioli, or as the basis of sweet dishes. In London I can buy it fresh every Friday from my Continental grocer. Mature Parmesan never gets 'tacky' when cooked. Mozzarella, made from buffalo's milk, is used a lot, too, as it melts easily at a low temperature.

Tomatoes are a national stand-by, but personally I never tire of them. In Nemi, a village near Rome, I was fascinated to see long trails of tomatoes hanging in great red clusters to dry in the sun on the warm walls of the houses. Someone told me that these dried tomatoes are made into blocks of tomato concentrate for use in the winter. Most stores sell tins and tubes of it, and it is extremely useful in the kitchen. I prefer the tubes as they are less wasteful.

Maria's personal coaching was important to me, because it showed me the difference between restaurant and home cooking. The ideal is to strike a happy balance between the two. One needs to market and cook in a country to get an insight into its gastronomic philosophy. In Italy there are a great many classic dishes, but in general the cooking remains individualistic and regional.

Italians grow peaches, apricots and figs, besides the more usual northern European fruits. Their wild strawberries are some of the most exquisite I have ever eaten. Perhaps they taste even better when one buys them in small handwoven baskets from peasant women standing by the roadside. In the woods women and children pick and fill huge baskets with mushrooms and other edible fungi.

Introduction

There are many species, and people are not afraid to eat them. A lot of them are dried, especially the large and golden 'procini'. The Tuscans cook the fresh 'procini' in a delicious way, stuffed with chopped garlic, onion and parsley and baked in olive oil—a simple, full-flavoured dish.

The Italians enjoy enormously all the bounties which a wonderful climate provides, and meat, game and fish are as good as the crops. They have a nice habit in some restaurants of bringing platters of raw fish or meat, to let the customer take his pick.

There are innumerable festivals celebrating saint's days and local events, and to celebrate food and wine as well. I especially liked the chestnut festival at Segni. This takes place about 21st October and to me it was a wonderful sight: the bar full of locals drinking wine or coffee and noisily gossiping and gesticulating, while a young pig was turning on a spit in the open—people bought a slice on a piece of bread and wandered round eating the hot meat inelegantly.

Throughout Italy they eat a great quantity of chestnuts because they know how nourishing they are. They make soups with them, use them as vegetables, and also make sweets with them, including their wonderful 'marroni confetti'—marrons glacés. These and their crystallized fruits are exported all over the world.

The grape grows everywhere, and there is a very wide span of wines: the light delicate wines of Frascati, lauded by Horace; Orvietto from Umbria, one of the most renowned and ancient; the dark-red, sparkling Lambrusco di Sorbara, with its tantalizing hint of violets; and the flinty-flavoured coarser wine of Venetia Julia . . .

In the autumn grape-harvest, donkeys and mules work as hard as the people. Huge panniers are straddled across their backs and filled to overflowing. They struggle up the steep cobbled roads to the wine presses. Everything is urgent. Enormous barrels are scrubbed clean in the streets, ready to hold the new wine.

Everywhere in due season men, women and children are busy tilling, tending, gathering, transporting and preserving the gifts of nature which are the foundation of the Italian 'cucina'.

Italy from North to South

Here are some of the specialities from the eighteen provinces of Italy. Some of them can only be eaten where they originate as they depend on local food and local cooks, but their mouthwatering splendour may tempt you to tour. Recipes are given for dishes marked with an asterisk.

PIEDMONT. This is a rich region and good food is abundant. Meat is excellent, and there is plenty of game. Rice is cultivated in the Po Valley. Fruit grows well, and the large yellow peaches are wonderful. The famous white truffles from Alba, which are really brown, are used in many dishes, especially with turkey, and sometimes fine slivers are sprinkled over risottos. There are various ways of cooking chestnuts, and Turin is world-famed for its confectionery. Cooking is mainly done in butter and garlic is plentifully used.

LOMBARDY. This is a lush and fertile country and the grape grows everywhere. Many well known dishes come from here, including all the recipes 'alla Milanese'. There is an unusual tripe dish (*Busecca), Hollow Bone Stew (*Osso Bucco), plenty of cooked rice, salame, wonderful butter and cheese, and the famous nougat (*Torrone di Cremona). As in Piedmont, polenta is one of the staple foods.

TRENTINO. The food has been influenced by Germany and Austria, there are German-type sausages and Apple Strudel. Meat is often stuffed. The fish from the lakes is outstanding. The fruit is superb.

VENETIA. Vegetables and fruit abound and there is an unusual

Italy from North to South

red-leafed salad (radicchio) which looks rather like a reddish corn salad—its bitter flavour goes well with roasts. Special dishes are Rice and Peas cooked together (*Risi e Bisi) and Liver and Onions (Fegato alla Veneziana).

VENETIA JULIA. Home of the delectable San Daniele ham. There are also fish soups and onion pasties, and the Austrian influence is traced in the *Goulash, and the Veal Escalopes (Wienerschnitzel).

LIGURIA. The sea-food is outstanding and used in a spicy fish soup (*Burrida) and shell-fish soups. A huge mixed salad is called *Cappon Magro. The great speciality is the basil, garlic, nut and oil sauce (*Pesto), served with soups and pasta dishes. Figs are stuffed with almonds or walnuts, and the tangerines from San Remo are juicy and sweet.

EMILIA-ROMAGNA. Bologna, which is one of the principal towns in this province, gives its name to a great number of dishes. Various types of pasta are made here—tagliatelle, tortellini and cappelletti; these are flat not hollow. The famed Parma ham (Prosciutto di Parma), Mortadella, stuffed pig's trotters (Zampone), and Parmesan cheese are made here, too.

TUSCANY. Florentine steaks from the superb Tuscany cattle are renowned throughout Italy, and Chianti is known everywhere. There is a special way of cooking fresh kidney beans in a 'flask',— a special bean-pot in which the beans keep all their flavour. They are served from the 'flask' and this dish is called 'fagioli al fiasco'. The beans are also cooked with sage, garlic and tomatoes. The delicious fruity spiced cake (*Panforte di Siena) is made in this region.

THE MARCHES. Fish caught in the Adriatic is full of flavour and the fish stews are excellent. Sucking pig is roasted on a spit and flavoured with rosemary and garlic. Veal is often cooked with

Italy from North to South

white wine. There are also large pasties, rather like Cornish pasties, filled with meat and the buffalo cheese, Mozzarella.

UMBRIA. Umbria has no coastline, but there is good fish from Lake Trasimene. Quite a lot of macaroni is made here, and salame. Dried figs are stuffed with almonds, and plums are dried as well. The black truffles from Norcia are full of flavour, and Norcia is also the place for wonderfully smoked hams and meats.

LAZIO. There are many specialities in this province: roast milk-fed lamb; stewed lamb's head and Lamb's Offal (*Coratella di Agnello); oxtails cooked with tomatoes and celery. Goat, too, is often served, and so are snails, globe artichokes and wild asparagus. Food is flavoured with herbs, spices and vinegar.

ABRUZZI. Food is very varied here. Near the coast one has fish soups and fried fish; inland, all parts of the pig are cooked and eaten. Excellent potatoes are cultivated. Olive oil is full-flavoured and good. Sweets are made with dried figs, and the famous sugared almonds come from Sulmona.

CAMPANIA. Plenty of egg plants and pimientos, and the tomato crops up in many dishes. Specialities include the spicy tomato sauce (*Pizzaiola), *Neapolitan Pizza, all kinds of pasta, a fish fry (*Fritto Misto di Pesce), the famous Rice Timbale (*Sartù), stewed mussels, and mussels cooked with spaghetti.

APULIA. This region has the longest coastline, so that, of course, there are plenty of fish dishes. Oysters and mussels from Taranto are outstanding and there are numerous ways of cooking them. Pasta is often baked. Other dishes are stuffed aubergines, and roast kid (*Capretto Al Forno). Fruit crops are good and the scented melons (popone) from Brindisi are superb.

BASILICATA. Ginger is the universal spice here and it goes into many of the dishes. Vegetable soups make a good foil for the vigorous

Italy from North to South

food. Smoked meat and sausages are plentiful and hare is jugged in a rich sauce.

CALABRIA. The trout caught in the Silva river are delicious. Macaroni is cooked with ricotta; pork is roasted with spices and bay leaves. The highly seasoned sausages are extremely popular. The olive oil is delicately flavoured, and the oranges are very fine.

SICILY. Fruit, vines and vegetables all grow well on this island. Tuna fish and swordfish are caught off the Ionian coast, and the fish dishes here are amongst the best in Italy. Marvellous sauces are made, to go with the fish and pasta dishes. Fruit is crystallized here and the ices are quite outstanding.

SARDINIA. Fish is exceptionally good. There is also plenty of game, and the wild boar is smoked to make an exciting ham. Blackbirds and thrushes are wrapped in myrtle leaves and gently roasted (Taccula). Saffron flavours many dishes. The shepherds here eat a special kind of bread called carta di musica. Fruit of all kinds grows well.

Herbs

LE ERBE ODOROSE

BASIL (*ocimum basilicum*) BASILICO

Basil, also known as Sweet Basil, is one of the most fragrantly perfumed herbs. It was popular in the seventeenth century in England and was used to flavour Fetter Lane sausages, a favourite food of that period. It is used a lot in Italy, especially in Genoa, where they say they grow the best. Italians add it to soups, salads, tomato sauces and it makes the 'pesto', that wonderful concoction of basil and grated Parmesan or Sardo cheese. It goes well with gnocchi and all forms of pasta.

BAY LEAVES (*laurus nobilis*) ALLORO, LAURO

A native of the Mediterranean, it also grows well in England. The leaves have been used in cooking for centuries in both savoury and sweet dishes. They have a piquant aroma. In Italy, as in France and England, they are put in soups, stews and marinades. Also good in custards and milk puddings.

FENNEL (*foeniculum vulgare*) FINOCCHIO

This is the herb for fish and fish sauces. It looks a little like cow parsley but the flowers are bright yellow. It has an aniseed flavour. The leaves, finely chopped, can be added to sauces, and fish is often grilled on the dried stalks. In Shakespeare's day the English used to cook it with eels. The dried seeds are used, too, and can be used when the fresh leaves are not available. There seems to be a little confusion about fennel because the vegetable, *foeniculum azoricum*, or Dwarf Fennel, is not the root of the herb but a separate plant. It has the same aniseed flavour and is eaten raw and cooked,

Herbs

but it is much better eaten raw. It is grown extensively in Italy and known as Florence Fennel.

GARLIC (*allium sativum*) AGLIO

There are two principal varieties, white and pink. The pink-tinged 'cloves' are smaller than the white. One of the oldest of herbs, known to the Egyptians and Hebrews, and surely one of the most useful. The Italians use it rather less than the people of Southern France. It goes into soups, stews, stuffings and sauces.

JUNIPER (*juniperus communis*) GINEPRO

The dried berries are used in cooking. They have a most unusual flavour rather suggesting a pinewood. They are used to make gin, and in cooking have a great affinity with the game who eat them.

MINT—SPEARMINT OR GARDEN MINT (*mentha viridis*) MENTA VERDE

There are many varieties of mint, some of which grow only in England, but spearmint is the one mainly used in the kitchen. There is an especially fragrant wild mint which grows around Rome and the Romans use it quite a lot in their cuisine to flavour soups, salads and fish.

OREGANO OR WILD MARJORAM (*origanum vulgare*) ORIGANO

This is, with basil, perhaps the most popular herb of Italy, and flavours soup, fish, pasta, pizzas and stews. It has a more pungent flavour than

SWEET MARJORAM (*origanum majorana*) MAGGIORANO

PARSLEY (*petroselinum sativum*) PREZZEMOLO

The universal herb, widely used in England, France and Italy for flavour, and to give colour. It is used in soup, omelettes, stews, stuffings and sauces.

Herbs

ROSEMARY (*rosmarinus officinalis*) ROSMARINO
A native of the Mediterranean, but it has been grown in England ever since Saxon times, though it is rarely used by the English in cooking. It has a strong, pervasive, almost gingery flavour, and a little goes a long way. Definitely an acquired taste. The Italians use it a lot, especially with sucking pig and lamb.

SAGE (*salvia officinalis*) SALVIA
A native of the Mediterranean. Used quite often in Italy to flavour veal, and in Lombardy it is used in fish dishes. In England we use it for stuffings with veal, duck and goose, and it marbles Derby sage cheese. The fresh leaves are so much nicer than the dried ones. It is a flavour I personally dislike, but a finely chopped leaf or two in a green salad is pleasant.

SAFFRON (*crocus sativus*) ZAFFERANO
Saffron is made from the dried stigmas of a type of crocus. It has always been expensive because about 70,000 stigmas are needed to make a pound of saffron. It was the most popular herb in England in the Middle Ages and was probably brought to England by the Romans. In some parts of Italy it is added to fish soups, and it colours and flavours the famous Milanese Risotto. It can be used in powder form, but it has a better and stronger taste if the dried stigmas are infused in a little water, which extracts the colour and flavour.

TARRAGON (*artemisia dracunculus*) SERPENTARIA OR DRAGONCELLO
One of the herbs used as 'fines herbes'. Much more widely used in France than in Italy. It flavours Tartare, Bearnaise and Ravigote sauces.

THYME (*thymus vulgaris*) TIMO
Not used much in Italy, but occasionally in stews. It is much more popular in France.

Spices

SPEZIE

※※※※※※※※

CINNAMON (*cinnamonum zeylanicum*) CANELLA
Cinnamon is the dried bark of the tree and can be used in 'sticks' or powdered. The best comes from Ceylon. It is used in Italy mainly for cakes and puddings, and with game.

GINGER (*Zingiber officinale*) ZENZERO
Ginger comes from the rhizome of the plant. One of the first Oriental spices known in Europe. Pliny and Marco Polo mention it. It is used in powder form, or in pieces known commercially as 'races' or 'hands'. The fine stem ginger preserved in syrup comes from mountains in China.

CLOVES (*caryophyllus aromaticus*) GAROFANO
The dried unopened flower bud is the part used in cooking, either whole or ground. The Italians add cloves to a beef stew and they are also one of the spices used in making the Panforte di Siena (see page 166).

CORIANDER (*coriandrum sativum*) CORIANDRO
Coriander was brought to England by the Romans. The dried seeds have a very pleasant odour. Apparently when they are green, the smell is rather unpleasant. Used in Italy with lamb, pork and fish.

MACE AND NUTMEG (*myristica fragrans*) NOCE MOSCATA
The nutmeg is the kernel and the mace the husk. Both of these are used in cooking. Widely used in Italy, especially with spinach

Spices

dishes (just as in England we like a dusting of nutmeg on brussels sprouts), and also in spiced cakes.

VANILLA (*vanilla planifolia*) VANIGLIA

The indispensable flavouring for ices, chocolate, cakes and many other sweets. The vanilla pods are far superior to the essence. They can be steeped in milk for milk puddings, custards, and so on, or vanilla-flavoured sugar can be made by putting a pod in a closed container of sugar.

Note

Recipes are mainly for 4 people.

Quantities of herbs and spices are suggested but take into account their freshness and your taste.

The quantity of oil will also depend on personal preference.

Sizes of tins will vary according to shape and depth. As a rough guide a 7-inch square tin (or a 8 in. ×6 in. rectangular one) will hold approximately as much as a round one 8 in. in diameter—i.e. a round tin should be 1 in. larger than a square one, but depth, too, must be taken into consideration.

Hors d'œuvre

ANTIPASTI

※※※※※※

Italian Pork Products	*Salumerie*
Artichoke Hearts in Olive Oil	*Carciofi Sott'Olio*
Aubergines in Tomato Sauce	*Caponatina*
Fried Cheese and Anchovy Sandwiches	*Crostini di Mozzarella con Acciughe*
French Bean Salad	*Insalata di Fagiolini*
Cucumber Salad	*Insalata di Cetriolo*
Mixed Salad	*Insalata Mista*
Haricot Beans with Tuna Fish	*Fagioli Toscani con Tonno*
Eggs with Tuna Fish Mayonnaise	*Uova Tonnate*
Raw Mushroom and Prawn Salad	*Insalata di Funghi e Gamberi*
Tomatoes Stuffed with Tuna Fish	*Pomidori Ripiene di Tonno*
Fennel	*Finocchio*
Potato Salad (1)	*Insalata di Patate*
Potato Salad (2) with Italian Dressing	*Insalata di Patate*
Potato and Tuna Fish Salad	*Insalata di Patate con Tonno*
Red Pimiento Salad	*Insalata di Peperoni*
Pimientos with Anchovies	*Peperoni con Acciughe*
Tomato Salad	*Insalata di Pomidoro*
Fried Stuffed Olives	*Olive Ripiene Fritte*
Raw Parma Ham with Melon or Figs	*Prosciutto di Parma e melone o Fichi*

Hors d'oeuvre

ANTIPASTI

On the Continent people rarely begin their mid-day meal with the main dish but serve appetizers first—in France hors d'oeuvre and in Italy antipasti. The Italians at home often have a few slices of sausage, black olives and anchovy fillets for a simple beginning.

They have some outstanding combinations such as a slice of raw ham—(prosciutto di Parma or San Daniele)—with sun-ripened figs, or melon or butter. Butter is seldom served with a meal except with ham and salame.

They serve exquisitely fresh vegetables dressed with olive oil and lemon juice or vinegar; delicate broad beans, finely sliced raw artichokes, green peas, raw mushrooms, fennel, and many others.

Together with the Germans, the Italians are the best sausage makers in the world. They have a tremendous variety of salame with quite different flavours. Several of these are obtainable in Soho, and in many large stores and delicatessen shops.

Then there is Buttàriga (caviar made from grey mullet eggs), and Uova di Tonno (dried, salted tuna fish eggs).

Salads, too, often begin a meal, as well as being served after the main course and so I have included them in this section.

Sometimes the Italians eat hot antipasti, such as small pizzas or crostini. Crostini are rounds of bread with different toppings; they are gently fried in oil until they are crisp and brown. They can be made with cheese and anchovies, mussels or other shellfish, ham or mushrooms—the choice is limitless.

One can also buy tins of antipasti, containing small pieces of mixed vegetables and fish, but personally I find them far too vinegary.

ITALIAN PORK PRODUCTS AND SAUSAGES

SALUMERIE

COPPA. Cured shoulder of pork served cut in thin slices.

COTECHINO. A large spiced pork sausage which has to be boiled. It is eaten hot, cut in thick slices. An essential part of a genuine Bollito (Italian Boiled Dinner) (see page 101).

MORTADELLA. A large sausage served cut in thin slices. The best comes from Bologna and is made from pork. Other types may be a mixture of pork, including pig's head, and veal, tripe, even donkey! It is usually flavoured with coriander and white wine and occasionally with pistachio nuts. Personally I find this a tasteless sausage. It is available in Soho and in many continental and delicatessen shops.

PANCETTA. Cured, rolled pork belly. Served cut in thin slices and eaten raw. It is cheaper than prosciutto but does not compare in flavour.

PROSCIUTTO CRUDO. This ham is served raw, either alone, or with melon, ripe figs or butter. It should be sliced wafer thin. The best comes from Parma and San Daniele near Trieste. The flavour is unique and much more delicate than hams of our curing. I think the ham from San Daniele is the best raw ham I have ever eaten. It is very expensive, and can be bought in Soho. It is available in tins at many shops; this tinned ham is good, but the flavour is not at all the same.

SALAME. In Italy most regions, and even towns, make their own special variations. A number of these are imported and are on sale in Soho and in continental shops elsewhere.

Hors d'oeuvre

MILAN SALAME. Made with equal quantities of pork, pork fat and beef, all finely chopped, and flavoured with garlic, white wine and pepper. It is one of the most usual commercial kinds. Served cut in thin slices.

GENOA SALAME. Made from 50 per cent veal, 20 per cent pork and 30 per cent pork fat. It is strongly flavoured. Served cut in thin slices. In Genoa they like to eat it with very young raw broad beans and ewe's milk cheese (the Sardo cheese of Sardinia).

ZAMPONE. Made of a mixture of pork which is stuffed into pig's trotter skins. It needs to be cooked before it is eaten. It should be soaked overnight, then put in cold water, brought slowly to the boil and simmered gently for 3–4 hours, according to size. They usually weigh about 3–4 lb.

ARTICHOKE HEARTS IN OLIVE OIL CARCIOFI SOTT'OLIO

If it is not easy to find very young, tender artichokes, use the tinned ones; they are quite excellent.

½ tin of artichoke hearts
3 tablespoons olive oil
salt, pepper and lemon juice to taste
½ bay leaf
½ tablespoon white wine

Drain the artichoke hearts well. Mix the oil, lemon juice, pepper, salt and wine together. Add the bay leaf. Pour the mixture over the artichokes. Leave them to marinate for 1 or 2 hours before serving, turning them over once or twice so that they are impregnated with the dressing.

Hors d'oeuvre

AUBERGINES IN TOMATO SAUCE CAPONATINA

2 *large finely-sliced aubergines*	2 *tablespoons chopped stoned black*
½ *large sliced onion*	*olives*
1 *chopped clove of garlic*	1 *tablespoon capers*
olive oil for frying	2 *tablespoons wine vinegar*
1 *8-oz. tin of Italian tomatoes*	1 *tablespoon sugar*
1 *small chopped head of celery*	*pepper and salt*

Fry the onion and garlic in the oil until they begin to soften. Add the aubergines and fry until they begin to brown. Add the tinned tomatoes and celery, olives and capers. Cover and cook very gently until the celery is tender. Dissolve the sugar in the vinegar, add it and season to taste. Continue to cook for 15 minutes, stirring occasionally. Serve cold.

FRIED CHEESE AND ANCHOVY SANDWICHES
CROSTINI DI MOZZARELLA CON ACCIUGHE

4 *slices of white bread,*	*pepper*
crusts removed	*olive oil, or butter, for frying*
8 *anchovy fillets*	
4 *thin slices of Mozzarella, Bel*	
Paese or Gruyère cheese	

Cut the slices of bread in half. Put a slice of cheese on one half, sprinkle with pepper, criss-cross with anchovy fillets and top with the other half. Fry the sandwiches gently in hot oil, or butter, until brown. Do not turn them over until the cheese has melted and stuck the slices together. Then turn, and brown the other side.

FRENCH BEAN SALAD INSALATA DI FAGIOLINI

1 *lb. French beans*	*pepper and salt*
1 *chopped clove of garlic*	*lemon juice*
olive oil	

Break off the ends of the beans. String the beans if necessary. Boil them in slightly salted water; do not overcook. Drain well, then

Hors d'oeuvre

chill. Mix together olive oil, garlic, pepper, salt and lemon juice to taste. Toss the beans in the dressing when you are ready to serve them.

CUCUMBER SALAD INSALATA DI CETRIOLO

1 large cucumber	chopped fresh basil or parsley
oil	pepper and salt
vinegar or lemon juice	

Do not peel the cucumber. Wipe it and cut into very thin rounds. Season with oil, vinegar or lemon juice, pepper and salt, and chopped basil or parsley.

MIXED SALAD INSALATA MISTA

1 mild onion cut into rings	2 hard-boiled eggs cut into rings
3 large sliced tomatoes	pepper and salt
1 small diced cucumber	2/3 oil to 1/3 vinegar
1 small tin of tuna fish	1 tablespoon chopped fresh basil or mint
2 chopped celery stalks	
stoned black olives	

Mix all the ingredients together, except the olives and eggs. Dress with oil and vinegar. Use the olives and eggs to decorate.

HARICOT BEANS WITH TUNA FISH FAGIOLI TOSCANI CON TONNO

In Tuscany, where this dish comes from, fresh beans are used, but it can be made with dried haricot beans.

1 lb. fresh haricot beans or ½ lb. dried beans soaked overnight	olive oil
8-oz tin of best-quality tuna fish in oil	1 small mild onion cut in thin rings
pepper and salt	chopped fresh basil or parsley

Cook the beans gently. When they are tender, drain well. Mix

Hors d'oeuvre

with plenty of olive oil and the onion slices, add pepper and salt to taste and leave to cool. To serve, arrange chunks of tuna fish on top, including the oil, and sprinkle with chopped basil or parsley.

EGGS WITH TUNA FISH MAYONNAISE UOVA TONNATE

4 hard-boiled eggs cut in half   *pepper and salt*
  lengthwise   *capers for garnishing*
tuna fish mayonnaise (see page 154)   *finely-chopped parsley*

Remove the egg yolks carefully and mix them with the tuna fish mayonnaise, adding pepper and salt to taste. Pile this mixture into the egg whites, decorate with capers and sprinkle with finely-chopped parsley.

RAW MUSHROOM AND PRAWN SALAD INSALATA DI FUNGHI E GAMBERI

This is very like the famous Swedish West Coast Salad. When I wrote about it over ten years ago, people were quite shocked at the idea of eating raw mushrooms. Do try them—they are quite delicious. Choose the freshest cultivated mushrooms you can find.

½ lb. mushrooms   *1 tablespoon lemon juice*
½ lb. cooked shelled large prawns   *pepper*
4 tablespoons olive oil

Wipe and slice the mushrooms, including the stalks. Mix the olive oil with the lemon juice and pepper and pour it over the mushrooms. Leave to marinate for an hour or so. When ready to serve, line a salad-bowl, or individual plates, with crisp lettuce leaves. Mix the mushrooms and prawns together and arrange on the lettuce.

Hors d'oeuvre

TOMATOES STUFFED WITH TUNA FISH POMIDORI RIPIENE DI TONNO

4 *large tomatoes*
2 *chopped hard-boiled eggs*
1 *small tin of tuna fish*
1 *teaspoon capers*
2 *tablespoons stiff mayonnaise*
pepper and salt
chopped fresh basil, parsley or marjoram

Cut a slice from the top of each tomato, then scoop out some of the inside. Mix this with the eggs, fish, capers, mayonnaise and chopped basil, parsley or marjoram, and season to taste. Fill the tomatoes with this mixture. Put the tops back on the filled tomatoes. Serve chilled.

FENNEL FINOCCHIO

Use the bulbous root of Florentine fennel for this. It is on sale in large stores and many greengrocers.

Wash the fennel in cold water. Drain it well. Make a dressing with olive oil, freshly ground black pepper and salt to taste. Dip the fennel in the dressing and eat it in your fingers. It can also be served at the end of a meal.

POTATO SALAD (1) INSALATA DI PATATE

On the Continent one can buy potatoes for a purée, potatoes for frying, potatoes for potato salad—in fact each variety has its special function. To make a good potato salad one really needs firm, waxy ones, new or old according to season, that will not break up easily. Steam or boil them gently and do not overcook.

6 *medium-sized potatoes*
1 *chopped mild onion, or chopped shallots*
pepper and salt
olive oil
lemon juice or wine vinegar
chopped parsley

Steam or boil the potatoes in their skins. Drain well as soon as they are cooked. Remove the skins as soon as you can handle them, then cut the potatoes in rounds. Sprinkle with pepper and

Hors d'oeuvre

salt, add the onion and dress with plenty of olive oil and a little lemon juice or wine vinegar. Garnish with chopped parsley.

POTATO SALAD (2) (WITH ITALIAN DRESSING) INSALATA DI PATATE

4–5 medium-sized potatoes
1 large mild onion sliced in rings
4 chopped anchovies
1 pimiento cut in strips
2 hard-boiled eggs cut in circles
a few black and green olives
lettuce leaves
Italian dressing (see below)
pepper

Steam or boil the potatoes in their skins. Remove the skins and cut the potatoes into rounds while they are still warm. Mix together the potatoes, onion, anchovies and pimiento. Toss the lettuce in some of the dressing and arrange the leaves in a large bowl. Pour the rest of the dressing on the potatoes, then pile the mixture on top of the lettuce. Decorate with circles of hard-boiled eggs and black and green olives.

For the Italian Dressing

1 chopped clove of garlic
1 tablespoon chopped fresh basil, tarragon, mint or parsley
pepper and salt
2 tablespoons olive oil
1 teaspoon caster sugar
lemon juice

Pound the garlic with the salt, pepper, sugar and chopped herbs until smooth. Gradually add the olive oil, mixing all the time. Add lemon juice to taste.

POTATO AND TUNA FISH SALAD INSALATA DI PATATE CON TONNO

4–5 medium-sized potatoes
1 finely-sliced onion
1 small tin of tuna fish in oil
pepper and salt
4–5 tablespoons olive oil
wine vinegar
capers
chopped parsley

Hors d'oeuvre

Boil the potatoes gently in their skins, do not let them break up. Drain them, remove the skins and slice the potatoes into a bowl. Add the onion, pepper, salt, oil and a little wine vinegar and mix together. When ready to serve, break up the tuna fish and mix it in carefully. Decorate with capers and chopped parsley.

RED PIMIENTO SALAD INSALATA DI PEPERONI

2 red pimientos
3 large firm sliced tomatoes
radishes
pepper and salt
olive oil

Remove the seeds and membranes from the pimientos. Cut the pimientos into strips and the radishes into circles. Add the tomatoes, with pepper and salt and plenty of olive oil.

PIMIENTOS WITH ANCHOVIES PEPERONI CON ACCIUGHE

4–5 pimientos (red, yellow and green)
2 chopped cloves of garlic
pepper and salt
4 tablespoons olive oil
butter
3 chopped anchovy fillets
chopped parsley

Cut the pimientos in half lengthwise; remove seeds and membranes. Put the pimientos in a shallow fireproof dish; season each half with garlic, oil, anchovy fillets, pepper and salt; dot with butter. Bake in a moderate oven (350°F–375°F) for about 30 minutes or until the pimientos have softened but are not at all squashy. Serve cold, sprinkled with chopped parsley.

TOMATO SALAD INSALATA DI POMIDORO

Try to get really large tomatoes for this dish.

large ripe sliced tomatoes
1 large mild sliced onion
olive oil
pepper and salt
chopped fresh basil or parsley

Arrange the sliced tomatoes and onion on a large shallow dish.

Hors d'oeuvre

Cover with plenty of olive oil and season to taste. Garnish with chopped basil or parsley.

FRIED STUFFED OLIVES OLIVE RIPIENE FRITTE

These are very fiddling to do, but if you have plenty of time and patience they are worth trying.

large green olives	*nutmeg*
finely-minced chicken	*1 beaten egg*
finely-minced ham	*oil for frying*
finely-minced anchovies	*short-crust pastry*
freshly-ground pepper	

Stone the olives carefully. Mix together the chicken, ham, anchovies, pepper and nutmeg and bind with the egg. Stuff the olives with this mixture. Roll out the pastry thinly; cut it into circles large enough to enclose the olives completely; damp the edges and press well together. Fry in hot oil until lightly brown. Serve hot or cold.

RAW PARMA HAM WITH MELON OR FIGS
PROSCIUTTO DI PARMA E MELONE O FICHI

4 slices thinly-sliced Parma ham   *4 slices of melon or fresh figs*

Serve a slice of ham and a slice of melon to each person. Or, and even better to my mind, whenever you can get really fresh ripe figs serve these instead of the melon. The sweetness of the figs contrasts admirably with the flavour of the ham.

Soups
MINISTRE

Beef Broth	*Brodo di Manzo*
Chicken Broth	*Brodo di Pollo*
Consommé with Pesto	*Brodo al Pesto*
Pavia Soup	*Zuppa alla Pavese*
Ragged Egg Soup	*Stracciatella*
Bean Soup	*Zuppa di Fagioli*
Green Soup	*Zuppa di Verdura*
Florentine Minestrone	*Minestrone alla Fiorentina*
Rice and Pea Soup	*Risi e Bisi*
Chestnut Soup	*Zuppa di Castagne*
Genoa Minestrone	*Minestrone Genovese*
Milan Minestrone	*Minestrone Milanese*
Noodle Soup with Chicken Livers and Peas	*Pasta in Brodo con Fegatini e Piselli*
Tripe Soup from Lombardy	*Busecca Lombardi*
Fish Soups	*Zuppe di Pesce*
Genoese Fish Stew	*Burrida*
Rimini Fish Soup	*Brodetto alla Rimini*

Soups
MINESTRE

The Italians begin most evening meals with soup and they have developed a wonderful selection. They make strong consommés (brodo) which can be the basis of soups or be served on their own. These can have miniature pasta shapes cooked in them to give body, such as acini di pepe (peppercorns), alfabeto (alphabet), diamanti (diamonds), farfalline (butterflies) and stelle (stars). Stracciatella is made by stirring raw beaten eggs into the simmering broth till they look like floating streamers.

Ministre is the general name for thick meat and vegetable soups, dating from the medieval stockpots in monastery and castle. The best known now are the minestrone (large ministre). These turn up in different forms all over Italy. What they contain depends largely on what is available. They are mainly vegetable soups cooked in a meat stock: a satisfying blend of chopped vegetables, pasta or rice and plenty of grated Parmesan cheese. Sometimes in hot weather they are served cold, and very refreshing they are.

Ministre can also be made from a single vegetable. There are minestra di spinaci (spinach soup), minestra di cavolfiore (cauliflower soup) and dried bean and lentil minestre.

All regions have their own specialities. In Genoa they add their famous 'pesto' (pounded garlic, basil, oil and Sardo cheese). In Rome they add the chopped wild mint which grows profusely in the countryside round about.

Fish soups are flavourful, colourful and exciting. They are always surprising and different, as they are a blend of locally caught fish, but they are invariably good. Many of the fish soups and minestrone are so hearty that they are a meal in themselves.

As so many Italian soups start with a beef broth or chicken

Soups

broth basis, I am giving recipes for both. But if you have neither the time nor the inclination to make them, there are good tinned consommés on the market, or beef and chicken bouillon cubes.

BEEF BROTH BRODO DI MANZO

1½–2 *lb. shin of beef*	2–3 *chopped carrots*
a beef marrow bone	4 *chopped tomatoes*
3 *quarts water*	2 *chopped celery stalks*
1 *large chopped onion*	1 *teaspoon salt*

Put the beef and bone into cold water, bring to the boil, skim, then add the salt. Now add the chopped vegetables and simmer gently for 2 hours. Strain into a basin. When cool, remove the fat. If you want a more concentrated broth, boil it quickly until it has reduced by half.

CHICKEN BROTH BRODO DI POLLO

1 *fresh prepared chicken (broiler or boiler)*	2 *chopped celery stalks*
giblets, wing tips and feet	3 *large chopped tomatoes*
2 *chopped onions*	1 *teaspoon salt*
2 *chopped carrots*	*pepper*
	3 *quarts water*

Wash the giblets; scald the feet and scrub them. Do use the feet; they make the broth much more gelatinous. You will have to ask the butcher to let you have them as they are usually thrown away. Put the chicken and giblets in a heavy saucepan, add the water and bring slowly to the boil. Remove any scum, then add the vegetables, salt and pepper. Cover and simmer gently until the chicken is tender. The time will depend on the age of the chicken (1½–2½ hours). As soon as the chicken is cooked, remove it and keep it hot to be served as the main course. Strain the broth. Correct the seasoning. Use as required.

Soups

CONSOMMÉ WITH PESTO BRODO AL PESTO

1½ *pints chicken or beef broth*
2 *tablespoons pesto (see page 154)*
1 *oz. soup pasta (stars, rings, alphabet, etc.)*

Heat the broth. Cook the pasta in it and when it is tender, stir in the pesto. Serve at once.

PAVIA SOUP ZUPPA ALLA PAVESE

8 *small round slices of bread*
butter for frying
2 *pints broth*
4 *eggs*
grated Parmesan cheese
pepper and salt

Fry the bread in butter until crisp and golden brown on both sides. Bring the broth to the boil. Put 2 slices of bread in each flat soup plate; break the eggs and slide one gently into each soup plate; sprinkle grated cheese on top. Pour the boiling broth over the eggs; spoon the broth over the eggs to cook them. Serve very hot. If you like your eggs very well cooked, poach them first in the broth before putting them in the soup plates.

RAGGED EGG SOUP STRACCIATELLA

2 *eggs*
1 *quart chicken or beef broth*
1 *heaped tablespoon fine semolina*
pepper and salt
2 *tablespoons grated Parmesan cheese*

Beat the eggs, semolina and cheese together. Add 2–3 tablespoons of the cooled broth and stir to mix. Heat the rest of the broth; when it is nearly boiling, add the egg mixture slowly, stirring all the time. The eggs form threads from which the soup gets its name.

BEAN SOUP ZUPPA DI FAGIOLI

½ *lb. haricot beans soaked overnight in 1 quart water*
½ *lb. diced salt pork*
1 *finely-chopped onion*
1 *finely-chopped clove of garlic*
3 *chopped tomatoes*
1 *chopped stick of celery*
pepper and salt
oil for frying
chopped parsley

Soups

Cook the salt pork, onion, garlic and celery in hot oil until they begin to brown, then add the tomatoes, beans, water, pepper and salt. Simmer gently until the beans are very well cooked. The time will depend on the type of bean and whether it is the new season's or the last (anything from 1½–3 hours). Serve sprinkled with the chopped parsley.

GREEN SOUP ZUPPA DI VERDURA

1 lb. washed, chopped spinach	2 tablespoons olive oil
1 lb. shelled green peas	1 quart white stock
4 or 5 coarsely-chopped leeks	pepper and salt
1 chopped Cos lettuce	chopped parsley
1 tablespoon chopped mint	

Heat the oil and cook the leeks in it until they begin to soften. Add the spinach, lettuce and mint; cook and stir for 2–3 minutes. Heat the stock and add it with the peas. Simmer until the vegetables are well cooked, then put them through a vegetable mill, or sieve them. Correct the seasoning. Reheat, and serve sprinkled with parsley. This soup is served really thick, but if you want it thinner dilute it with more stock.

FLORENTINE MINESTRONE MINESTRONE ALLA FIORENTINA

½ lb. dried haricot beans soaked overnight	1 bay leaf
1 chopped onion	sprig of rosemary
1 chopped leek	1 chilli
¼ small chopped red cabbage	1 tablespoon olive oil
3–4 chopped tomatoes	1 tablespoon butter
pepper and salt	1 quart stock or water
	small triangles of fried bread

Heat the oil and butter together and fry the onion and leek till golden-brown. Add the stock or water, the beans, cabbage, tomatoes, bay leaf, rosemary and chilli, and salt and pepper to taste (the

Soups

amount will depend on whether you are using water or stock). Simmer gently, tightly covered, until the beans are well cooked. Add more stock or water if necessary. Correct the seasoning. Serve in soup plates on top of the fried bread.

RICE AND PEA SOUP RISI E BISI

This very thick soup, almost a risotto, comes from Venice.

1½ lb. shelled green peas
¾ lb. Italian rice
1 chopped onion
1 quart chicken broth
pepper and salt
1 tablespoon olive oil
1 tablespoon butter

Melt the butter and oil together. Add the onion and fry it until it has softened. Add the rice; stir and cook for 5 minutes. Add the peas; stir and cook for 2–3 minutes. Add the hot stock; simmer gently for 15–20 minutes or until the rice is cooked. Correct the seasoning. Serve hot, with grated Parmesan cheese.

CHESTNUT SOUP ZUPPA DI CASTAGNE

¾ lb. whole chestnuts, or a tin of unsweetened chestnut purée
2 chopped onions
1 chopped carrot
1 chopped celery stalk
1 bay leaf
pepper and salt
1 quart stock or water
oil for frying
croûtons of fried bread

If you are using whole chestnuts, nick them at one end and leave them in a moderate oven for 10–15 minutes. When they are not too hot to handle, remove the shells and skins with a sharp knife. Heat the oil and fry the onions, carrot and celery until they have softened, then add the stock or water and the whole chestnuts (or chestnut purée). Simmer gently until the chestnuts break up. Put the vegetables and chestnuts through a vegetable mill, or rub them through a sieve. Reheat them in the stock, correct the seasoning and serve with croûtons of fried bread.

Soups

GENOA MINESTRONE MINESTRONE GENOVESE

4 oz. haricot beans soaked overnight
1 large chopped carrot
1 chopped onion
2 chopped celery stalks
¼ small cabbage finely chopped
1 chopped young turnip
4 oz. chopped French beans
a handful of shelled green peas
3 oz. short macaroni
2 pints broth or water
pepper and salt
4 tablespoons pesto (see page 154)
olive oil for frying

Begin by cooking the beans in the broth or water for 1–1½ hours. Heat the oil in a heavy pan and cook the onion, celery, turnip, and carrots until they begin to soften, then add them to the beans. Cook for 1 hour, then add the cabbage, French beans, peas and macaroni and cook for 20–25 minutes. Correct the seasoning. Add the pesto, stir it well in and cook for 5 minutes without boiling.

MILAN MINESTRONE MINESTRONE MILANESE

1 chopped onion
1 chopped clove of garlic
2 chopped celery stalks
2 chopped carrots
1 large diced peeled potato
¼ small cabbage finely chopped
1 small chopped courgette or zucchini
1 large handful of fresh green peas
1 teaspoon chopped sage
1 tablespoon chopped parsley
1 tablespoon tomato concentrate
2 pints broth or water
2–3 oz. diced green back bacon
pepper and salt
a little olive oil for frying
grated Parmesan cheese
4 oz. well-washed rice

Heat the oil in a large heavy saucepan. Add the onion, garlic, carrots, celery and bacon and cook until they are softened. Only a little oil is needed as the fat from the bacon will soon run. Add the stock or water, the rest of the vegetables, salt if necessary and pepper. Stir in the tomato concentrate and cook gently for 40 minutes. Add the rice, sage and parsley; cook for 20 minutes. Serve with grated cheese.

Soups

NOODLE SOUP WITH CHICKEN LIVERS AND PEAS
PASTA IN BRODO CON FEGATINI E PISELLI

2 pints chicken broth
6 chopped chicken livers
12 oz. cooked green peas
4–5 oz. fine pasta

butter
pepper and salt
grated Parmesan cheese

Wash and chop the livers and fry them in butter for 2–3 minutes. Cook the pasta in boiling salted water for 5 minutes; drain well. Heat the broth, then add the pasta, peas and the livers. Heat for 2–3 minutes. Add pepper and salt if necessary. Serve with grated Parmesan cheese.

TRIPE SOUP FROM LOMBARDY BUSECCA LOMBARDI

This soup from Lombardy is an excellent way of serving tripe and is thick enough to serve as a stew. The tripe one gets from the butcher's is usually blanched and prepared for cooking.

1 lb. tripe cut in small pieces
3 chopped onions
2 chopped carrots
1 chopped leek
2 chopped celery stalks
½ small chopped cabbage
6 oz. dried beans soaked overnight

3 finely-chopped fresh sage leaves
a handful of chopped parsley
1 tablespoon tomato concentrate
2 oz. chopped smoked bacon
pepper and salt
1 tablespoon flour
1 tablespoon olive oil

Cook the chopped vegetables in hot oil. Sprinkle in the flour and let it brown, but not burn. Pour in the stock, add the beans, tripe, bacon and sage, bring to the boil, add seasoning to taste, stir in the tomato concentrate. Cover the saucepan and cook very gently for 2½–3 hours. Serve hot sprinkled with parsley.

FISH SOUPS ZUPPE DI PESCE

Most of these are really fish stews and, like the French bouillabaisse, a meal in themselves. In England, unfortunately, we are not able to get many of the types of fish caught in the Mediterranean and Adriatic. We can compromise, however and make a first-rate dish

Soups

without loss of flavour, but it will be different. If you have a fisherman in the family, any freshwater fish can be used—it does not matter how small or how bony. Most of these soups or stews need to be highly seasoned.

GENOESE FISH STEW BURRIDA

4–5 lb. *assorted fish, including small lobster, conger eel, mackerel, whiting and squid*

For the Broth

1 *chopped onion*
1 *chopped carrot*
2 *chopped sticks of celery*
2 *chopped cloves of garlic*
sprigs of parsley
3 *chopped anchovy fillets*
2 *lb. peeled, chopped tomatoes*
4 *oz. chopped mushrooms*
pepper and salt
1 *dessertspoon chopped basil*
olive oil
1 *gill fish stock made from fish heads and trimmings*

Fry the onion in hot oil till softened and golden. Add the carrot, celery, garlic, parsley sprigs and anchovy fillets and cook for 5–6 minutes. Add the mushrooms and tomatoes; season with pepper, and salt if necessary, then add the fish stock and the squid cut in pieces. Simmer gently for 30 minutes. Add the rest of the fish cut in fair-sized slices. Simmer for 20–25 minutes until the fish is cooked.

RIMINI FISH SOUP BRODETTO ALLA RIMINI

4–5 lb. *assorted fish, including shelled prawns, shelled mussels, halibut or turbot, red mullet, eel, and sole or bass*

For the Broth

1 *sliced onion*
2 *cloves of garlic*
1 *lb. peeled, chopped tomatoes*
1 *gill dry white wine*
1 *dessertspoon chopped oregano or marjoram*
1 *tablespoon chopped parsley*
bay leaf
pepper and salt
a good pinch of saffron
slices of fried French bread

Soups

Put the fish heads, trimmings and prawn shells into a large saucepan. Add the onion, garlic, tomatoes, parsley, oregano, bay leaf, pepper, salt and white wine. Simmer for 30 minutes, then remove all the fish trimmings and rub the broth through a sieve. Now add the eel, cut in 2-inch lengths, and let it cook for 10 minutes; then add the rest of the fish, cut in convenient pieces as necessary, and cook for 20 minutes. Ten minutes before the fish is cooked, pour a little of the broth on to the saffron, and mix, then return it to the saucepan. Arrange the fish on a dish and serve the broth separately, poured on top of the fried bread.

Pasta

Some Types of Pasta
How to Cook Pasta
Basic Dough for Tagliatelle, Lasagne and Ravioli

Spaghetti with Eggs and Bacon	*Spaghetti alla Carbonara*
Spaghetti with Meat Sauce	*Spaghetti al Sugo di Carne*
Noodles with Pounded Basil	*Pasta al Pesto*
Spaghetti with Oil and Garlic	*Spaghetti all'Olio e Aglio*
Spaghetti Bolognese	*Spaghetti Bolognese*
Noodles with Chicken Livers	*Tagliatelle con Fegatini di Pollo*
Spaghetti Syracuse Style	*Spaghetti alla Siracusa*
Spaghetti with Mushrooms	*Spaghetti all'Ortica*
Vermicelli with Anchovies	*Vermicelli con Acciughe*
Vermicelli with Mussels	*Vermicelli con le Cozze*
Spaghetti with Meat Balls	*Spaghetti con Polpette*
Baked Green Lasagne	*Lasagne Verdi al Forno*
Macaroni with Ricotta	*Maccheroni con Ricotta*
Baked Macaroni	*Maccheroni al Forno*
Noodles with Hare Sauce	*Fettucine con la Lepre*
Ravioli	*Ravioli*
Fillings for Ravioli	
Meat Filling	*Ripieno di Carne*
Cheese Filling	*Ripieno di Ricotta*
Spinach Filling	*Ripieno di Verde*
Cannelloni	*Cannelloni*

Pasta

The mixing together of flour and water to make palatable food has been known from time immemorial. Although one immediately thinks of spaghetti and macaroni as essentially Italian, the Japanese and Chinese were making forms of vermicelli and spaghetti as early as 3000 B.C.

Throughout history the Italians have made 'pasta' their staple diet. Napoleon said that an army marches on its stomach. The Roman Legionaries conquered the then known world and yet they ate scarcely any meat. These tough fighting men of old marched and fought on a diet consisting mainly of these earliest forms of pasta.

Through the ages the making of pasta has evolved to give us the very finest 'capelli d'angelo' (angel's hair) to the very broad macaronis—smooth, ridged, hollow, flat or solid—and large squares or tubes of paste filled with meat and vegetables.

The Italians have special dishes for each type, and the shape, size and texture does affect the taste. There are many Italian, Continental and large stores in England that sell many different types, and it is well worth while experimenting and not just sticking to noodles, spaghetti or macaroni. The best pasta is made from durum wheat, known as semolina. Some have eggs added (pasta all'uovo). Others are coloured green with spinach or red with tomatoes.

One should learn to eat spaghetti or noodles properly. They should never be cut with a knife, but should be eaten with a spoon and fork. Take the spoon in the left hand, the fork in the right, twirl the spaghetti round the fork against the spoon, and you will find you have a neat mouthful and will not have to suck up long strands noisily à la Charlie Chaplin.

Pasta

Outside Italy pasta is often served with the meat course instead of potatoes, but in Italy it is always a separate course.

SOME TYPES OF PASTA

There are over 300 different kinds of pasta, many of which vary only slightly, or have different names in different regions. I am listing only a few of the more readily obtainable types. They are arranged in descending order of size.

FLAT PASTA

Lasagne. Sometimes coloured green with spinach, or pink with tomato. Up to 2 inches wide.

Fettuccine or Tagliatelle. About ¼ inch wide and often made with eggs. Often called noodles. Sometimes available in twined bundles or 'nests'.

Taglierini and Linguine. The narrowest of the flat noodles.

ROUND, SOLID PASTA

Spaghetti. The thickest and best known. Cylindrical.

Vermicelli. The next thickest.

Spaghettini, Capellini, Fideline. Decreasingly slender solid 'spaghetti'.

Capelli d'angelo (Angel's hair). The most slender of all.

TUBULAR PASTA

Cannelloni. Very broad 3–4-inch tubes, which are stuffed. (See also Stuffed Pasta below.)

Ditali. Very broad short macaroni.

Ziti. Narrower macaroni. Usually short lengths.

Macaroni. Long lengths as a rule.

Tubetti. Narrower macaroni.

Bucatini. The narrowest macaroni.

SHAPED PASTA (Often used in soup)

Alfabeto. Tiny letters of the alphabet.

Pasta

Conchiglie. Shells.
Farfalline, Farfalle. Butterflies.
Lumache. Snails.
In addition there are stars, rings, squares and grains.

STUFFED PASTA
Cannelloni. Large stuffed tubes.
Ravioli. Square cushions.
Agnolotti, Capelleti, Tortellini. Variations of ravioli.

HOW TO COOK PASTA

Allow 3-4 oz. per person. Use a really large saucepan and cook the pasta, without a lid, in plenty of boiling salted water. To each 1 lb. of pasta allow 1 gallon of boiling water and 1 heaped tablespoon of salt. The water must be boiling really fast or the pasta will stick and parts be uncooked. Do not break up long lengths of spaghetti and other kinds, but put it upright in the saucepan; as it heats, it becomes pliable and will slip into the water. Stir once or twice to prevent sticking. Cooking time varies considerably with the type of pasta. It may be from 6 to 12 minutes. Try a piece before draining the pasta. It should be 'al dente'—firm to the tooth, as the Italians say—but completely cooked. Like all simple things it must be cooked to perfection. So often it is served either as a tasteless mushy mess or so undercooked that one can taste the raw flour.

If you can get freshly-made noodles—often on sale in Italian shops in Soho—or make your own, you will find that they have a different taste and texture. They do not need cooking for as long as the dried.

I have a pair of large-toothed tongs, which I bought in Italy, for serving spaghetti, noodles, and so on. Failing this, use two forks. When your pasta is cooked, drain it thoroughly, put it in a warmed dish or bowl and serve it on really hot plates, as it does cool quickly.

Pasta

BASIC DOUGH FOR TAGLIATELLE, LASAGNE AND RAVIOLI

Tagliatelle
1 lb. sifted flour
1 teaspoon salt

3–4 eggs
a little water

Sift together the flour and salt, then put the flour on a large board or smooth unpainted surface. Make a depression in the centre, beat the eggs well and pour them in, adding about a tablespoon of water. With a spoon, gradually incorporate the flour into the liquid. When about half the flour has been mixed in, start kneading with the hands until all the ingredients are well mixed. Continue kneading, pulling the dough out to make it elastic, until the dough is smooth; this will take about 10 minutes. Leave for 30 minutes. Divide the dough into three or four pieces. Roll out each piece on a floured board with a well floured rolling-pin—the dough should be paper thin. This is a bit difficult, but practise makes perfect!

Sprinkle the rolled-out dough with a little flour. Roll up each piece and cut it into strips $\frac{1}{2}$–$\frac{3}{4}$ inch wide. Separate the strips, unroll them and leave to dry out for about 10 minutes. Cook them in plenty of boiling salted water until tender.

To make Lasagne Verdi (green lasagne). Add 2–3 oz. very well drained spinach purée to the above ingredients, omitting the water. Work the spinach well into the flour and eggs, and knead until the dough is thoroughly elastic. Should the dough be too soft, add a little more flour; if it is too stiff, add a little water. Cut the dough into very wide strips (about 2 inches) when it has been rolled out as thinly as possible. Separate the strips, unroll them and leave to dry out for about 10 minutes. Cook according to the directions given in the recipe for Baked Green Lasagne (see page 56).

For Ravioli. Make the tagliatelle dough, then roll it into large squares or oblongs and cut small rounds or squares as desired. Follow the directions given in the section on ravioli (see page 58).

Pasta

SPAGHETTI WITH EGGS AND BACON SPAGHETTI ALLA CARBONARA

This is one of my favourite ways of serving pasta.

1 lb. spaghetti or noodles boiled in the usual way
4 oz. rashers of fat bacon, cut in small pieces
4 slightly-beaten eggs
freshly-ground pepper
2 tablespoons finely-chopped fresh oregano or marjoram, or
1 teaspoon dried oregano or marjoram
grated Parmesan cheese

While the spaghetti is cooking, gently fry the bacon. Drain the spaghetti well and put it back in the saucepan. Now quickly add the beaten eggs and mix them in, then add at once the bacon, pepper and oregano or marjoram; stir them in and serve straight away. Have plenty of grated Parmesan cheese to sprinkle on top. Serve a crisp green salad afterwards and end with some fresh fruit for a perfect meal.

SPAGHETTI WITH MEAT SAUCE SPAGHETTI AL SUGO DI CARNE

1 lb. freshly-cooked spaghetti
Butter to mix with spaghetti
grated Parmesan cheese

For the Sauce

2 finely-chopped onions
1 chopped clove of garlic
¾ lb. minced lean beef
1 bay leaf
pepper and salt
1 lb. skinned fresh tomatoes, or equivalent tinned
2 tablespoons chopped parsley
1 tablespoon butter
3 dessertspoons olive oil

Heat the butter and olive oil together and cook the onions and garlic until they soften. Add the meat, pepper and salt; stir and cook for 7–8 minutes. Now add the bay leaf, parsley and tomatoes. Squash the tomatoes with a wooden spoon as they heat. Simmer the sauce for 25–30 minutes. Remove the bay leaf. Add plenty of butter to the spaghetti, mix it in, pour the sauce over the pasta and sprinkle with plenty of grated Parmesan cheese. Serve at once.

NOODLES WITH POUNDED BASIL PASTA AL PESTO

This delicious dish can be made with noodles, spaghetti, macaroni or any kind of pasta you like. Its incomparable flavour comes from the pounded fresh basil and there is really no substitute for this. I find basil grows very well in a window box.

1 lb. freshly-cooked pasta

For the Sauce, or Pesto

2 chopped cloves of garlic
2 good handfuls of basil leaves
1 oz. pine nuts
2 anchovy fillets

2 oz. grated pecorino cheese or Parmesan cheese
freshly-ground pepper
olive oil

Put the garlic, basil, anchovies, pine nuts and cheese into a large mortar or a thick bowl. Pound them thoroughly with a pestle until you get a thick smooth paste. Now gradually add enough olive oil, stirring well, to get a cream-like consistency. Serve the pesto on top of the pasta — each person can mix his own in. Hand round grated pecorino or Parmesan.

SPAGHETTI WITH OIL AND GARLIC
SPAGHETTI ALL'OLIO E AGLIO

This dish is strictly for garlic lovers.

1 lb. freshly-cooked spaghetti
8 chopped cloves of garlic
6 tablespoons olive oil

3 chopped anchovies
chopped parsley
pepper

Heat the olive oil and cook the garlic until it begins to brown. Pour it over the spaghetti. Add the anchovies, parsley and pepper. Mix in thoroughly. Serve at once.

Pasta

SPAGHETTI BOLOGNESE

This Bolognese sauce, or ragù as it is properly called, goes well with most types of pasta.

1 lb. freshly cooked spaghetti

grated Parmesan cheese

For the Sauce, or Ragù

8 oz. minced lean beef
5–6 diced rashers of green back bacon
1 finely-chopped onion
1 finely-chopped clove of garlic
1 finely-chopped carrot
1 small stick of celery finely chopped
1 dessertspoon tomato concentrate
½ pint stock, or use a bouillon cube
pepper, salt, nutmeg to taste
butter for frying

Brown the bacon rashers in hot butter. Add the chopped vegetables; let them soften and brown. Add the minced beef; stir it in. Cook for 2–3 minutes. Add the tomato concentrate to the hot stock, stir to mix, and add it to the meat mixture. Add the seasoning. Cover the pan and simmer very gently for 30–40 minutes. Pour the mixture over the pasta. Hand round grated Parmesan cheese.

NOODLES WITH CHICKEN LIVERS TAGLIATELLE CON FEGATINI DI POLLO

1 lb. freshly-cooked noodles
4 tablespoons olive oil
5–6 chopped chicken livers
4 oz. sliced mushrooms
2 tablespoons tomato concentrate
1 gill hot water
pinch of cayenne pepper
pepper and salt
grated Parmesan cheese

Heat the olive oil and fry the chicken livers for 5 minutes. Add the mushrooms and cook for 10 minutes. Add the tomato concentrate, diluted with the hot water, the cayenne pepper, pepper and salt. Mix all together and pour the mixture over the noodles. Sprinkle with Parmesan cheese.

Pasta

SPAGHETTI SYRACUSE STYLE SPAGHETTI ALLA SIRACUSA

1 lb. freshly-cooked spaghetti
4 tablespoons olive oil
2 chopped cloves of garlic
6 large peeled tomatoes
1 small finely-diced aubergine
1 large sliced pimiento
12 chopped stoned black olives
1 tablespoon capers
1 teaspoon chopped marjoram
3 finely-chopped anchovies
freshly-ground pepper
salt if necessary

Brown the garlic in the hot oil. Add the aubergine, pimiento, and tomatoes and cook for about 30 minutes until the aubergine is cooked. Add the olives, capers, pepper, anchovies and marjoram. Cover the pan and simmer for 15 minutes. Correct the seasoning. Serve the mixture poured over the spaghetti.

SPAGHETTI WITH MUSHROOMS SPAGHETTI ALL'ORTICA

1 lb. freshly-cooked spaghetti
½ lb. thinly-sliced mushrooms
2 tablespoons olive oil
freshly-ground pepper, salt
1 tablespoon chopped parsley
1 teaspoon lemon juice

Cook the mushrooms in the hot oil until they are tender, then add the pepper, salt, parsley and lemon juice. Mix them into the cooked spaghetti and serve at once.

VERMICELLI WITH ANCHOVIES VERMICELLI CON ACCIUGHE

1 lb. freshly-cooked vermicelli
1 finely-chopped onion
2 finely-chopped cloves of garlic
6 chopped anchovies
1 tablespoon chopped parsley
freshly-ground black pepper
3 tablespoons butter
3 tablespoons oil
grated Parmesan cheese

Cook the onion and garlic in the hot oil and butter. Add the chopped anchovies; let them warm through. Add the chopped parsley and the pepper. Stir to mix, then pour the mixture over the vermicelli. Sprinkle plentifully with Parmesan cheese.

Pasta

VERMICELLI WITH MUSSELS VERMICELLI CON LE COZZE

1 lb. freshly-cooked vermicelli	1–1½ lb. skinned, chopped tomatoes
2 quarts mussels	pepper and salt
1 finely-chopped onion	chopped parsley
2 chopped cloves of garlic	2–3 tablespoons olive oil

Wash and clean the mussels thoroughly. Put them in a large pan with about 1 gill of water and salt to taste. Cook briskly for 5–6 minutes, shaking the pan now and again. As soon as the shells open, remove from the heat. Drain, and remove the mussels from the shells. Cook the onion and garlic in the hot olive oil. Add the tomatoes; cook them a little and press them with a wooden spoon. Add pepper and salt. Simmer gently for 30–40 minutes. Add the mussels and parsley, let them heat through, then pour the mixture over the vermicelli. Grated cheese is not served with this dish.

SPAGHETTI WITH MEAT BALLS SPAGHETTI CON POLPETTE

1 lb. freshly-cooked spaghetti	2 tablespoons grated Parmesan cheese
½ lb. minced veal	1 teaspoon finely-chopped basil
½ lb. minced pork	2 slightly-beaten eggs
1 cup stale fine white breadcrumbs	olive oil for frying
pepper and salt	

Mix the meat with the breadcrumbs. Add pepper, salt, the cheese and the basil, and bind with the eggs. Form into small balls, about the size of ping-pong balls. Heat the olive oil and brown the meatballs on all sides.

For the Sauce

1 chopped onion	pepper and salt
1 chopped clove of garlic	dash of cayenne pepper
1 large tin of tomatoes	olive oil
1 small tin of tomato concentrate	

Cook the onion and garlic in the hot oil. Add the tomatoes; when they are hot, add the tomato concentrate. Stir to mix.

Pasta

Add seasoning to taste. Put the meat-balls in the sauce and cook gently for 50–60 minutes. Pour the sauce over the spaghetti and arrange the meat-balls around. Serve with grated Parmesan cheese.

BAKED GREEN LASAGNE LASAGNE VERDI AL FORNO

Lasagne verdi are large flat noodles coloured green. Preferably they are coloured with spinach. They can be anything from ½ inch to 2 inches wide. They are usually boiled in salted water for 5–6 minutes, or longer, then baked in the oven.

½ lb. green lasagne
½ pint Bolognese sauce (see page 53)
½ pint Béchamel sauce

grated nutmeg
1½–2 oz. grated Parmesan cheese

Add plenty of grated nutmeg to the Béchamel sauce. Keep this and the Bolognese sauce hot while preparing the lasagne. Cook the lasagne in boiling salted water, for 5–6 minutes if freshly made; if dried ones are used, they will take about 10 minutes. Drain well. Grease a fireproof dish plentifully, put a layer of lasagne on the bottom, cover with a layer of the Bolognese sauce, then the Béchamel sauce, continue in this way. Finish with Béchamel sauce. Sprinkle Parmesan cheese on top. Bake in a moderate oven (350°F) for 30 minutes. Cut in squares to serve.

MACARONI WITH RICOTTA MACCHERONI CON RICOTTA

1 lb. freshly-cooked macaroni
½ lb. ricotta or other curd cheese
freshly-ground pepper
salt

½ teaspoon nutmeg
2 tablespoons chopped parsley
1 oz. butter
grated Parmesan cheese

Mix the ricotta, pepper, salt and nutmeg together with a wooden spoon until very smooth. Mix in the parsley. Add the butter to the cooked macaroni, then add the flavoured ricotta, and mix well in. Cover and leave for 2 minutes over a very low heat. Serve sprinkled with Parmesan cheese.

Pasta

BAKED MACARONI MACCHERONI AL FORNO

1 lb. macaroni	pepper, salt, nutmeg
1 pint Béchamel sauce	butter
grated Parmesan cheese	breadcrumbs fried in butter

Make the Béchamel sauce with 1½ oz. butter, 1½ oz. flour and 1 pint of milk. Add plenty of grated cheese and season to taste. Half cook the macaroni in boiling salted water, Drain it well. Put it in a greased baking-dish, then pour the sauce over and mix it well in. Sprinkle with more cheese and cover with the fried breadcrumbs. Put in a moderate oven (350°F) for 15-20 minutes. The top should be golden-brown.

Variations
Minced ham and hard-boiled eggs can be added to the sauce, or minced cooked chicken.

NOODLES WITH HARE SAUCE FETTUCINE CON LA LEPRE

1 lb. cooked noodles	1 blade of mace
2 chopped onions	1½ lb. hare
1 chopped carrot	1 small tin of tomatoes
2 chopped sticks of celery	1 wineglass Marsala or sherry
2 chopped cloves of garlic	½ pint hot stock
4 oz. sliced mushrooms	1 heaped tablespoon flour
4 diced rashers of streaky bacon	fresh or dried marjoram or thyme
freshly-ground pepper	to taste
salt	butter or oil for frying
a sprinkling of nutmeg	grated Parmesan cheese

Heat the butter or oil in a heavy saucepan. Add the onions, carrot, celery, garlic, pepper, salt, nutmeg and mace; fry for 9-10 minutes. Add the bacon; cook until the fat runs. Add the hare; let it brown. Add the mushrooms; cook for 1-2 minutes. Sprinkle in the flour; stir, and let it brown. Add the tomatoes, wine and stock. Sprinkle in the marjoram or thyme. Simmer gently for 1 hour. Remove the hare, take the meat off the bones and chop finely. Put the meat

Pasta

back into the sauce, stir and heat through. Serve the sauce poured over the noodles, and hand round grated Parmesan cheese.

RAVIOLI

Ravioli are tiny pouches filled with meat, cheese, vegetables and other delectable mixtures. Served with a spicy 'sugo' (sauce), or with grated cheese and butter, they make one of the most attractive entrées or an excellent main dish. They can be bought freshly made in many Italian shops, or deep-frozen or tinned; but they are fascinating and reasonably simple to make at home.

Agnolotti, a Turin variant, is served in the same way. Both agnolotti and ravioli can also be cooked in 'brodo' (consommé). They 'pop' in the mouth, making an ordinary soup adventurous.

Make the ravioli dough according to the basic recipe on page 50.

Divide the dough in two and roll out each half as thinly as possible. Have plenty of flour on the board and on the rolling-pin. The paste should be so thin that you can almost see through it. You should be able to get a 12-inch square from half the dough. Put it carefully on a clean cloth while you roll out the second piece in the same way.

Put teaspoonfuls of your chosen mixture about 1½–2 inches apart on one piece of the paste, damp it round the edges, lay the other piece of paste loosely on top, and with a sharp knife cut it into 1–1½-inch squares, or into rounds. Gently separate the ravioli, and press the edges well together so that the filling cannot come out while cooking. Cover with a floured cloth, to prevent them from drying out, until you are ready to cook them.

Bring a large saucepan of salted water to the boil. Put in a few ravioli at a time; if you put too many in, they will stick together. Cook them gently for 4–5 minutes. When they come to the top of the water they are cooked. Remove them carefully with a perforated spoon. Drain well and keep them warm in a well buttered or oiled fireproof dish while you cook the rest. Serve with melted butter and grated cheese, or with meat or tomato sauce (see pages 51, 151, and 152).

Pasta

FILLINGS FOR RAVIOLI

MEAT FILLING RIPIENO DI CARNE

½ lb. *finely-chopped minced cooked beef, veal, pork or chicken, or a mixture of 2 or 3 meats*

1 *well-beaten egg*
pepper, salt and nutmeg to taste
2 *tablespoons chopped parsley*

Mix all the ingredients well together. Put a teaspoonful of the mixture on each square or round.

CHEESE FILLING RIPIENO DI RICOTTA

½ lb. *ricotta or other curd cheese*
2 *tablespoons Parmesan cheese*

1 *well-beaten egg*
1 *tablespoon chopped parsley*

Mix all the ingredients well together. Put a teaspoonful of the mixture on each square or round.

SPINACH FILLING RIPIENO DI VERDE

4 oz. *well-cooked and drained spinach*

½ lb. *ricotta or other curd cheese*
pepper and salt

Mix all the ingredients well together. Put a teaspoonful of the mixture on each square or round.

CANNELLONI

Cannelloni are tubes of paste usually stuffed with meat, vegetables or cheese, like ravioli. They can be bought in Soho, freshly-made or in tins, or you can make your own.

Make the dough according to the basic recipe on page 50. Roll out the dough thinly and cut it into oblongs about 3 inches by 4 inches. Cook a few at a time in boiling salted water for about 5 minutes. Remove with a perforated spoon, drain well, let them cool. Put the chosen filling along the centre and roll up like a Swiss roll. Arrange the cannelloni in a greased fireproof dish, sprinkle with plenty of grated Parmesan cheese and dot with butter. Cover with meat or tomato sauce (see pages 51 and 151). Bake in a moderate oven (350°F) for 15–20 minutes.

Fillings for Cannelloni

Any of the ravioli fillings are suitable for Cannelloni. If liked, they can have very finely-chopped onion and garlic added.

Dumplings

GNOCCHI

Baked Dumplings	*Gnocchi al Forno*
Semolina Dumplings	*Gnocchi di Semolino*
Potato Dumplings	*Gnocchi di Patate*
Green Potato Dumplings	*Gnocchi di Patate Verdi*
Soup Dumplings Bolognese Style	*Passatelli alla Bolognese*
Romagna Spinach Dumplings in Broth	*Passatelli in Brodo*
Saffron Semolina Dumplings	*Maloreddus*
Piquant Sauce	*Salsa di Spezie*
Corn Meal	*Polenta*
Plain Boiled Polenta	*Polenta Bollita*
Baked Polenta	*Polenta al Forno*
Chicken Livers with Polenta	*Fegatini con Polenta*
Polenta Dumplings with Sauce	*Batuffoli al Sugo*

Dumplings
GNOCCHI

Italian dumplings (gnocchi) are very different from our soggy and often heavy dumplings which are sometimes served with boiled beef and carrots. They are light, small shapes and can be made with semolina, mashed potatoes, flour and cornflour, and formed into little sausages or cut into rounds, squares or diamonds. They make a good entrée or light supper dish. They can be poached in boiling salted water, or baked and served with melted butter and grated cheese, or served with a tasty sauce. Sometimes they are cooked in a consommé to make it more satisfying.

BAKED DUMPLINGS GNOCCHI AL FORNO

4 level tablespoons flour
4 level tablespoons cornflour
pepper and salt
a little grated nutmeg

2 oz. butter
1 pint milk
2 egg yolks
3 oz. grated Parmesan cheese

Sift the flour, cornflour, salt, pepper and nutmeg together. Melt the butter, gradually add the sifted flour and stir and cook until the butter is absorbed. Heat the milk and add it slowly, stirring all the time. Beat the egg yolks and add them; mix them in well, then add the cheese. Cook very slowly, stirring continuously until the mixture is thick and smooth. Spread it on a slightly wet flat surface and smooth with a wet knife until it is about $\frac{1}{2}$ inch thick. Let it cool completely, then cut it into circles about 1 inch in diameter. Put the gnocchi in a greased fireproof dish in overlapping layers. Bake in a moderate oven (375°F) for 15–20 minutes or until golden-brown. Serve hot.

Dumplings

SEMOLINA DUMPLINGS GNOCCHI DI SEMOLINO

4–5 oz. fine semolina
1 pint milk
1 teaspoon salt
freshly-ground pepper

grated nutmeg to taste
2 eggs
2 oz. grated Parmesan cheese
melted butter

Season the milk with the salt, pepper and nutmeg and bring it to the boil in a heavy saucepan. Dribble in the semolina, stirring constantly with a wooden spoon; when it is really thick (after about 10 minutes), remove from the heat. Add the beaten eggs and cheese. Pour the mixture into a well-greased shallow dish (approximately 10 × 8 inches) and smooth it with a wet palette knife; the mixture should be about ½ inch thick. Leave it until it is quite cool—to save time, it can be left to cool overnight. The next day cut the mixture into rounds, squares, oblongs or diamonds. Well-grease a shallow fireproof dish and put the gnocchi in, leaving a little space between each one. Pour melted butter on top, sprinkle with grated cheese. Bake in a moderately hot oven (375°F) until they are lightly browned.

POTATO DUMPLINGS GNOCCHI DI PATATE

2 lb. mashed potatoes without
 butter or milk
approximately ½ lb. flour

pepper and salt
2 beaten eggs
1 oz. butter

Add the butter, pepper, salt and eggs to the mashed potatoes and gradually add enough flour to make a workable dough. Roll it into a long thin roll with the hands. Cut off 1-inch pieces. Put a few at a time into boiling salted water. As soon as they float to the surface, then are cooked; this takes 3–4 minutes. Drain well. Serve with grated Parmesan cheese or a tomato sauce (pages 151, 152).

GREEN POTATO DUMPLINGS GNOCCHI DI PATATE VERDI

Make the mixture for potato dumplings as in the preceding recipe and add 8 oz. cooked, well-drained spinach purée; mix it in

Dumplings

y. Form into small balls and poach them in plenty of
lted water for about 15 minutes. Drain well and serve
ovy sauce.

nchovy Sauce

1 chopped onion
1½ oz. butter
4 finely-chopped anchovy fillets
4–5 peeled, chopped tomatoes

2 tablespoons water
freshly-ground black pepper
chopped parsley

Brown the onion in the hot butter. Add the anchovies, tomatoes, water and pepper. Cook gently for 20 minutes. Add the parsley and serve hot.

SOUP DUMPLINGS BOLOGNESE STYLE PASSATELLI ALLA BOLOGNESE

½ lb. finely-minced beef
1 large slice of bread, crusts removed
1 beaten egg

pepper and salt
grated Parmesan cheese

Soak the bread in a little milk, then squeeze out the moisture. Mix all the ingredients well together. Form into small balls. Poach them in soup for 15–20 minutes.

ROMAGNA SPINACH DUMPLINGS IN BROTH PASSATELLI IN BRODO

8 oz. well-drained, finely-chopped cooked spinach
2 tablespoons flour
1 beaten egg

pepper, salt and nutmeg to taste
2 tablespoons grated Parmesan cheese
1 quart strong chicken broth

Mix well together the spinach, flour, egg, cheese and seasoning. Form the mixture into small balls. Cook them in boiling broth for 5 minutes, then reduce the heat and simmer for 15–20 minutes.

Dumplings

SAFFRON SEMOLINA DUMPLINGS MALOREDDUS

In Sardinia, these semolina dumplings flavoured with saffron are served with a spicy sauce.

5 oz. semolina	a good pinch of saffron
1 pint milk	2 tablespoons grated pecorino or
pepper and salt	any other sharp cheese
2 beaten eggs	

Stir the saffron into the milk, add pepper and salt, stir and bring to the boil. Gradually add the semolina, stirring all the time until it thickens. Remove from the heat. Add the beaten eggs and stir in the grated cheese. Form the mixture into small balls and poach in plenty of boiling salted water for 15 minutes. Drain well and serve with a piquant sauce (see below) and grated cheese.

PIQUANT SAUCE SALSA DI SPEZIE

3 finely-diced bacon rashers	pepper and salt
1 chopped onion	a good pinch of ginger
1 chopped celery stalk	2 tablespoons wine vinegar
1 chopped clove of garlic	1 tablespoon Marsala
butter for frying	1 tablespoon capers
1 bay leaf	½ pint meat broth
2 cloves	

Heat the butter. Add the onion, bacon, celery and garlic. Cook until the onion has softened. Add the bay leaf, pepper and salt, ginger, wine vinegar, Marsala, and the broth. Simmer for 20 minutes. Add the capers and cook for a further 5 minutes.

CORN MEAL POLENTA

Corn meal (or maize flour) is sold in England in most Italian delicatessan shops and many supermarkets. It is bright yellow and can be fine or coarse. It is universally used in Northern Italy. It can be eaten with butter and grated cheese, or served with fish, meat and

Dumplings

poultry, and can be baked, boiled or fried. It is also used for making dumplings (gnocchi). In some parts of Italy it is always served with the small wild birds which are cooked without being drawn. A familiar sight, especially early on Sunday morning, is to see men cycling home with a string of small birds, mainly larks and thrushes, hung round their necks. I have never been able to eat this dish.

Nearly all the recipes for polenta begin with boiling it. Allow 1 quart of water and 2 heaped teaspoonfuls of salt to 1 lb. of polenta. If it is too thin, add a little more polenta gradually. If it thickens too much, add a little more boiling water. It must be stirred continually while it is boiling. If it is to be baked or fried afterwards, turn it on to a board, let it cool and set, then cut it with a knife.

PLAIN BOILED POLENTA POLENTA BOLLITA

8 oz. fine polenta
1 pint boiling salted water
pepper and salt

grated Parmesan cheese
butter

Sprinkle the polenta gently into the boiling water. Stir constantly, to prevent lumps, until it begins to thicken; then simmer gently for 30 minutes, stirring gently from time to time. Add the butter and cheese and correct the seasoning. Serve hot.

BAKED POLENTA POLENTA AL FORNO

Boil the polenta, as in the previous recipe, until it is very stiff. Remove from the saucepan and let it set on a smooth surface. Grease a fireproof dish, put in alternate layers of polenta and grated Parmesan cheese and bake in a hot oven (400°F) for about 20 minutes, it should be hot all through and the top brown. Serve with a brown or tomato sauce (see pages 150, 151 and 152).

Dumplings

CHICKEN LIVERS WITH POLENTA FEGATINI CON POLENTA

½ lb. chicken livers
3 diced bacon rashers
2 fresh sage leaves, or a pinch of dried sage
butter for frying
pepper and salt
½ pint chicken stock
1 lb. polenta
1–1½ pints boiling water
1 dessertspoon salt

Melt the butter. Cut up the chicken livers and add them with the bacon, pepper and salt. Let the livers and bacon brown, then add the stock and cook gently for 10 minutes. Keep hot. Pour the polenta gradually into the boiling salted water and cook until it leaves the sides of the pan (about 30 minutes). Now pour the polenta into a shallow serving-dish, put the chicken livers and gravy on top and serve at once.

POLENTA DUMPLINGS WITH SAUCE BATUFFOLI AL SUGO

8 oz. cooked polenta
1 pint meat sauce (see page 51)
grated Parmesan cheese
butter

When the polenta is cool, form it into small balls and arrange them in a buttered fireproof dish. Pour some meat sauce on top, next plenty of grated cheese, and continue until the polenta balls are used up. Top with small pieces of butter and more grated cheese. Bake in a hot oven until the top is a good sizzling brown. Serve hot.

Rice

RISO

Plain Risotto — *Risotto Bianco*
Milanese Rice — *Risotto alla Milanese*
Rice and Aubergines — *Riso e Melanzane*
Risotto with Mussels — *Risotto con Cozze*
Stuffed Rice Balls — *Arangini*
Rice Mould — *Sartù*
Rice and Chicken Livers — *Riso con Fegatini di Pollo*

Rice

RISO

In Italy, rice is just as much a staple as pasta, especially in the North where it is largely cultivated in the Po Valley. The Italians usually cook their rice slowly in stock; with this slow cooking it does not break up and become mushy. It is worth while using Italian rice, if possible, for their recipes. This is readily available in Soho and in many continental and delicatessen shops. Wash the rice in cold water, drain it, put it on a clean cloth, fold the cloth over and rub the rice; it is now ready for cooking. The quantity of rice really depends on whether it will be for a main dish or an entrée. Allow about 3 oz. per person, or about half a cupful. Cooking time varies with the quality of the rice; the better the rice, the longer it takes to cook, as it absorbs more liquid.

PLAIN RISOTTO RISOTTO BIANCO

12 oz. rice
1 medium-sized chopped onion
1 oz. butter

about 2 pints hot water
pepper and salt to taste
butter and Parmesan cheese

Fry the onion in hot butter until it becomes translucent; do not let it brown. Add the rice and stir it until it, too, is translucent. Now gradually add the hot water, letting some of it be absorbed before adding any more. Cook gently, stirring occasionally; when the rice is nearly cooked, stir more frequently to prevent sticking. When the rice is tender, it is cooked. Add butter, pepper and salt and grated Parmesan cheese. Serve at once, with more butter and cheese so that people can help themselves.

Rice

MILANESE RICE RISOTTO ALLA MILANESE

This is one of the best Italian rice-dishes, but it must be well made. There are several versions. In one the rice is cooked in chicken broth and white wine, flavoured with saffron and served with butter and grated Parmesan cheese. Another version has the marrow from beef bones added.

12–14 oz. rice
1 oz. butter
1 medium-sized finely-chopped onion
1½ pints–2 quarts chicken broth
3–4 dried saffron filaments, or a pinch of powdered saffron
a small wineglass of white wine
butter
grated Parmesan cheese
pepper and salt

Melt the butter in a heavy saucepan and cook the onion until it is translucent and lightly golden. Add the rice and stir gently over a low heat; when it has absorbed the butter, add the white wine and cook until it has almost evaporated. Now begin to add the hot broth, about half a pint at a time. Stir occasionally. The amount of broth added depends on the quality of the rice and how long it takes to cook. Dissolve the saffron in a little of the broth and stir it in well, so that the rice is evenly coloured. As soon as the rice is cooked, add a good knob of butter, with Parmesan cheese and pepper and salt to taste. Serve hot with extra Parmesan cheese on the side.

If you are going to add beef marrow, add about 1 oz. after the onion is cooked and before adding the rice.

RICE AND AUBERGINES RISO E MELANZANE

12 oz. cooked rice
1 large aubergine
1 medium-sized chopped onion
2 tablespoons tomato concentrate
½ pint stock
pepper and salt
4 thin slices of Bel Paese or Gruyère cheese
grated Parmesan cheese
1 dessertspoon chopped basil or parsley
olive oil

Rice

Cut the aubergine into thin rounds and fry lightly in hot oil until brown. Remove from the pan. Fry the onion until golden. Mix the tomato concentrate with the hot stock, add it to the onion, stir and cook for 5 minutes. Put a layer of rice in a greased fireproof dish, then put in a layer of aubergine, season with pepper and salt, put 2 slices of cheese on top, pour in half the stock, and continue with rice, aubergine, pepper, salt and sliced cheese. Pour in the rest of the stock. Sprinkle in the chopped basil or parsley and top with grated Parmesan cheese. Cook in a moderate oven for 30 minutes. Serve hot.

RISOTTO WITH MUSSELS RISOTTO CON COZZE

2 quarts cleaned mussels
3 chopped shallots
1 chopped clove of garlic
1 bay leaf
2–3 sprigs of parsley
1 tablespoon chopped parsley
pepper and salt

a pinch of saffron
a thin strip of orange peel
1 gill white wine
1 gill water
12 oz. uncooked rice
2 tablespoons olive oil

Make sure the mussels are quite clean and the little beard of seaweed removed. Soften the shallots and garlic in half the oil. Add the wine, water, parsley sprigs, bay leaf, orange peel, pepper and salt. Bring to the boil and cook for 5 minutes. Add the mussels, cook them until they open, then remove them immediately from the court bouillon and shell them as soon as they are cool enough to handle. Heat the rest of the oil in a large pan and put in the rice. Cook, stirring frequently, until the rice begins to colour. Gradually add the strained stock and saffron. Cook gently until the rice is done, adding more stock as it is absorbed. Add the mussels and chopped parsley; stir quickly; let the mussels heat through. Serve at once.

Rice

STUFFED RICE BALLS ARANGINI

12 oz. rice
8 oz. minced beef or veal
1 hard-boiled egg finely chopped
2 tablespoons grated Parmesan
   cheese
1 tablespoon chopped parsley
pepper and salt
beaten egg and fine brown
   breadcrumbs for coating
oil for deep-frying

Boil the rice in salted water until it is tender; drain well; bind with some of the beaten egg. Brown the meat in a little fat or butter, then add to it the cheese, parsley and hard-boiled egg. Form the mixture into small balls; coat it generously with the rice, so that it is completely enclosed. Dip in beaten egg, then in breadcrumbs, and fry in oil until lightly browned. Serve with a brown or tomato sauce (see pages 150, 151, 152).

RICE MOULD SARTÙ

This dish comes from Naples. A timbale of rice is filled with veal rissoles (polpette), turkey or chicken giblets, mushrooms and green peas. As it takes a long time to prepare, begin the day before: make the tomato sauce and cook the giblets and mushrooms, then you will only have to make the veal rissoles, cook the rice and peas, arrange the ingredients and cook the Sartù in the oven.

To cook the giblets and mushrooms

giblets from 1 turkey or 2 chickens
2 chopped onions
1 chopped carrot
1 chopped clove of garlic
¼ lb. sliced mushrooms
bay leaf
pepper and salt
water

Put the giblets (except the liver), onions, carrot, garlic and bay leaf in a saucepan, cover with water, add salt and pepper. Simmer gently for 2–3 hours. Add the liver and mushrooms and cook for a further 15–20 minutes. Remove the giblets, liver and mushrooms, then chop up the giblets and liver.

Rice

To make the tomato sauce

1 lb. skinned and quartered tomatoes
1 chopped onion
2 chopped cloves of garlic
3 finely-chopped bacon rashers
pepper and salt
chopped basil or parsley
oil for frying

Fry the onion and garlic in hot oil until the onion softens and becomes translucent. Add the bacon; cook for 3 minutes. Add the tomatoes, pepper and salt, and the basil or parsley. Cook, pressing with a wooden spoon now and again to extract the juice from the tomatoes. Simmer until the sauce is nice and thick.

To make the rissoles

8 oz. minced veal
2 slices of bread soaked in milk
2 beaten eggs
1 teaspoon chopped parsley
pepper and salt
oil for frying

Squeeze the bread dry. Mix all the ingredients together and form into baby rissoles. Fry in hot oil until they are brown all over. Keep hot.

To cook the rice

12 oz. rice   boiling salted water

Boil the rice until it is done (12–15 minutes). Drain well.

To assemble the Sartù

rissoles (see above)
4 oz. Bel Paese or Gruyère cheese (ideally the cheese should be Mozzarella)
8 oz. cooked green peas
grated Parmesan cheese
brown breadcrumbs
cooked giblets and mushrooms (see above)
cooked rice (see above)
tomato sauce (see above)

Grease a large soufflé or fireproof dish. Cover the bottom with breadcrumbs. Put in half the rice, then the giblets, mushrooms, rissoles and peas, and the cheese cut in small squares. Pour in a little of the tomato sauce. Put the rest of the rice on top. Pour in the

Rice

rest of the tomato sauce. Sprinkle with Parmesan cheese, cover plentifully with breadcrumbs, dot with butter. Cook in a moderate oven (375°F) for 30–35 minutes, when the top should be brown. Serve hot.

RICE AND CHICKEN LIVERS RISO CON FEGATINI DI POLLO

8 oz. rice
¾ pint chicken stock
a pinch of saffron
2 tablespoons grated Parmesan cheese
pepper and salt
1 lb. chopped chicken livers
3 tablespoons olive oil
chopped parsley

Heat the chicken broth, add the rice gradually, bring to the boil. Dilute the saffron with a little stock and stir it in. When the rice is just cooked, stir in the cheese. Correct the seasoning. Fry the livers in the hot oil for about 5 minutes. Put them in the middle of the serving-dish, arrange the rice round them and sprinkle with chopped parsley.

Pizzas

PIZZE

✼✼✼

Basic Pizza Dough
Pizza with Mussels   *Pizza con Cozze*
Four Seasons Pizza   *Pizza Quattro Stagioni*
Neapolitan Pizza   *Pizza Napoletana*
Franciscan Pizza   *Pizza alla Francescana*
Rustic Pizza   *Pizza Rustica*

Pizzas

PIZZE

I always enjoy watching pizza makers in the Pizzerias. They take a ball of dough, flatten it out, sprinkle it with oil and arrange a garnish dexterously in a matter of minutes. The decorated pizza is put on a special wooden shovel and pushed into the glowing pizza oven, which is wood-fired. The variety of toppings is almost endless: tomatoes, cheese, onions, garlic, anchovies, olives, shellfish, sausages, artichoke hearts, mushrooms and eggs are some of the things that are used to give an enormous selection of different pizze.

In a little while your pizza is served—crisp, full flavoured and very appetizing. To enjoy it to the full, you should eat it straight from the oven before it has had time to harden. Drink a glass of robust red wine with it and you have a real feast.

Some people will tell you that pizze can be made with shortcrust pastry; of course they can, but they are not at all the same. They can be made quite successfully at home, but they never get that unique taste which the glowing embers of the wood fire give them.

The pizza has spread along the coast into the South of France. Many of the bakers make huge squares which are cut into small pieces and sold individually. These mainly have the same ingredients on top, tomato, garlic, anchovies, cheese and olives—which makes the famous Neapolitan Pizza (Pizza Napoletana).

BASIC PIZZA DOUGH

8 oz. plain flour
¼ oz. fresh yeast, or
1 level teaspoon dried yeast

1 level teaspoon salt
1 gill lukewarm water

Pizzas

Sift the flour and salt on to a pastry board and make a well in the centre. Put the fresh yeast in the water, mix it and pour it on to the flour, gradually mixing it in. If using dried yeast, add 1 teaspoon of sugar to the lukewarm water; when it has dissolved, add the yeast and leave it until it froths. Knead the dough thoroughly, stretching it at the same time to make it smooth and elastic. Make the dough into a ball, put it in a lightly-greased bowl, cover with a damp cloth and leave it in a warm place to rise. It should have doubled in size in 60–70 minutes. Put the dough on a floured board; knead lightly. Halve the dough. Roll each piece into a disc about ¼ inch thick and 8 inches in diameter, or you can make one large disc. Put the rounds on an oiled baking-tray, leave room between them, then cover with your chosen topping. Bake in a hot oven (425°F) for 25–30 minutes, or until the dough is crisp and brown.

PIZZA WITH MUSSELS PIZZA CON COZZE

8 oz. pizza dough
1 lb. coarsely-chopped tomatoes
pepper and salt
olive oil

4 oz. thinly-sliced Mozzarella or Bel Paese cheese
½ pint mussels (when cooked and shelled)

Make rounds (discs) of dough as in the basic recipe. Arrange the topping ingredients on each pizza and sprinkle with olive oil. Bake in a hot oven (425°F) for 25–30 minutes.

FOUR SEASONS PIZZA PIZZA QUATTRO STAGIONI

8 oz. pizza dough
1 lb. roughly-chopped tomatoes
sliced cooked mushrooms
tinned artichoke hearts
cooked, shelled shrimps, prawns and mussels

pepper and salt
slices of Mozzarella or Bel Paese cheese
anchovy fillets
olive oil

Make one large round, using the basic dough recipe. Arrange the chopped tomatoes all over the surface. Each quarter should be different, so arrange the mushrooms on the first, the artichokes on the second, the shellfish on the third and on the last the cheese. Sprinkle with pepper, salt and olive oil; criss-cross with anchovy fillets. Bake in a hot oven (425°F) for 20–30 minutes. Serve cut, so that each person has a half of two quarters.

NEAPOLITAN PIZZA PIZZA NAPOLETANA

8 oz. pizza dough
1 lb. coarsely-chopped ripe tomatoes
9–10 anchovy fillets
stoned black olives
pepper and salt

5 oz. thinly-sliced Mozzarella or
 Bel Paese cheese
a sprinkling of marjoram or
 basil
olive oil

Cover the dough rounds with the tomatoes, arrange the anchovy fillets attractively on top, put the olives here and there and add the thin slices of cheese. Season with a little salt and plenty of pepper, sprinkle with the marjoram or basil, then sprinkle liberally with olive oil. Bake in a hot oven (425°F) for 20–30 minutes. The dough should be crisp and brown. Divide in halves or quarters according to appetites.

FRANCISCAN PIZZA PIZZA ALLA FRANCESCANA

8 oz. pizza dough
3 oz. sliced mushrooms
3 oz. diced ham
3 coarsely-chopped tomatoes

2 oz. finely-sliced Mozzarella or
 Bel Paese cheese
pepper and salt
olive oil

Cook the mushrooms in hot oil until they soften. Arrange them with the rest of the ingredients on the rounds of dough; sprinkle with olive oil. Bake in a hot oven (425°F) for 20–30 minutes.

RUSTIC PIZZA PIZZA RUSTICA

For the pastry
8 oz. plain flour
4 oz. lard
2 eggs

¼ teaspoon baking powder
½ teaspoon salt
cold water

Pizzas

Sift the salt and baking powder with the flour, rub the lard into the flour until it is like breadcrumbs, put the eggs in the centre of the mixture, mix them well in, then add enough cold water to make a soft dough.

For the Filling
1 *pint Béchamel sauce*
2 *egg yolks*
3 *oz. grated Parmesan cheese*
3 *oz. curd cheese*
3 *oz. cooked diced ham*
2 *hard-boiled eggs sliced thinly*
pepper and salt

Add the 2 egg yolks to the warm Béchamel sauce, stir to mix, then add the other ingredients. Divide the pastry in two. Roll it out to fit a shallow baking-dish, spread the filling on the first piece, moisten the edges and put the second piece of pastry on top: press the two edges well together so that the filling cannot come out. Bake in a moderate oven (350°F–375°F) for 40–45 minutes. Serve just warm.

Eggs
UOVA

Eggs with Lentil Purée	*Uova con pure di lenticchie*
Eggs Rossini	*Uova Rossini*
Eggs with Parmesan Cheese	*Uova alla Parmigiana*
Eggs with Chicken Livers	*Uova con Fegatini*
Florentine Eggs	*Uova alla Fiorentina*
Hard-boiled Eggs with Curd Cheese	*Uova Sode con Ricotta*
Omelettes	*Frittate*
Potato Omelette	*Frittata con Patate*
Pimiento Omelette	*Frittata con Peperoni*

Eggs

EGGS WITH LENTIL PURÉE UOVA CON PURE DI LENTICCHIE

4 rashers of lean bacon
4 eggs
4 tablespoons cooked lentil purée
pepper and salt
2 tablespoons melted butter

Fry the bacon lightly and arrange it in a buttered fireproof dish. Put the lentil purée on top, break in the eggs, pour the butter over and season to taste. Bake in a hot oven (420°F–440°F) until the eggs are set, or cooked to your liking.

EGGS ROSSINI UOVA ROSSINI

4 eggs
4 slices of pâté de foie gras or liver sausage
½ pint brown sauce (see page 150)
1 gill Marsala

Poach the eggs. Put each one on a slice of pâté. Add the Marsala to the brown sauce, heat and pour it over the eggs and pâté. Serve at once.

EGGS WITH PARMESAN CHEESE UOVA ALLA PARMIGIANA

4 eggs
4 tablespoons double cream
grated Parmesan cheese
pepper and salt
melted butter

You will need small individual ramekins for this. Heat the cream and when it is just boiling, put a tablespoonful into each ramekin. Break in the eggs, season to taste, add a good sprinkling of Parmesan and pour melted butter over. Bake in a hot oven (420°F–440°F), in a 'bain marie', until golden-brown.

Eggs

EGGS WITH CHICKEN LIVERS UOVA CON FEGATINI

4 *chopped chicken livers*
2 *tablespoons olive oil*
2 *tablespoons Marsala or sherry*
1 *tablespoon tomato purée*
1 *small chopped onion*
1 *chopped clove of garlic*
4 *eggs*
1 *tablespoon butter*
pepper and salt

Fry the onions and garlic in the hot oil until the onion is translucent. Add the livers; fry gently. Mix in the Marsala and tomato purée, season to taste, simmer slowly. Break the eggs into a buttered fireproof dish, pour melted butter over and cook for 10 minutes in a moderate oven (350°F–360°F). Add the livers and sauce; bake for 4 minutes longer. To enhance this dish, serve broccoli or asparagus tips with it.

FLORENTINE EGGS UOVA ALLA FIORENTINA

4 *eggs*
1 *lb. cooked spinach tossed in butter*
1 *oz. butter*
grated Parmesan cheese

Soft-boil the eggs for 4 minutes; shell them; arrange them on top of the spinach in a buttered fireproof dish. Cover them with Mornay sauce (see below), sprinkle with Parmesan and brown quickly in a very hot oven or under the griller.

For the Mornay Sauce

1 *oz. butter*
2 *tablespoons flour*
½ *pint milk*
2 *fluid oz. cream*
1½ *oz. grated Gruyère cheese*
1 *oz. grated Parmesan cheese*
pepper and salt

Melt the butter without letting it burn. Stir in the flour; when it is well mixed, add the milk slowly, stirring all the time with a whisk. Do this over a low heat. Continue stirring until the sauce bubbles gently. Season with pepper and salt to taste. Let the sauce reduce by about a third, then add the cream, Gruyère and Parmesan. Stir and cook for a few minutes.

Eggs

HARD-BOILED EGGS WITH CURD CHEESE UOVA SODE CON RICOTTA

4 hard-boiled eggs
½ lb. ricotta or other curd cheese
4 finely-chopped anchovy fillets
2 tablespoons grated Parmesan cheese
pepper and salt
a dash of nutmeg
flour
1 beaten egg
brown breadcrumbs
oil for deep-frying

Shell the eggs, cut them in half lengthwise and carefully remove the yolks. Mix them with the curd cheese, anchovies, Parmesan, pepper, salt and nutmeg. Now take each half egg white and build it up with the cheese mixture so that it looks like a whole egg. Lightly coat with flour, dip in beaten egg, then in breadcrumbs. Fry the 'eggs' in deep oil until they are as brown as the best eggs.

OMELETTES FRITTATE

The ancient Romans may not have invented the omelette, but the word in all probability came from them originally. They used to eat a mixture of eggs beaten with honey, cooked in an earthenware dish. This was called 'ova mellita'. The Italians may not mix their omelettes with honey now, but they have their own variations. Instead of folding the omelette over the filling, they usually mix everything into the eggs before they are cooked—much more like a pancake than an omelette.

POTATO OMELETTE FRITTATA CON PATATE

5 tablespoons mashed potatoes
4 beaten eggs
2 tablespoons grated Parmesan cheese
1 finely-chopped onion
pepper and salt
3 tablespoons olive oil

Mix the potatoes, eggs, cheese, pepper and salt together. Fry the onion in the hot oil until it is soft and transparent. Add the potato and egg mixture and cook briskly until it begins to brown. Reduce

Eggs

the heat and cook for 5 minutes, then turn the omelette and cook and let it brown on the other side. Chopped sausages can also be added if liked.

PIMIENTO OMELETTE FRITTATA CON PEPERONI

1 *red pimiento*
3 *tablespoons olive oil*
1 *crushed clove of garlic*
5 *eggs*
pepper and salt

Remove the seeds and membranes from the pimiento, cut it into narrow strips and fry it in hot oil until it softens and begins to brown. Add the garlic; cook for a minute or two. Beat the eggs lightly, season them, pour them into the frying-pan and stir to mix in the pimiento and garlic. Cook until the omelette is well set. Serve hot.

Fish

PESCE

Crawfish Fra Diavolo	*Arogasta alla Fra Diavolo*
Sicilian Couscous	*Cuscusu alla Siciliana*
A Fish Salad	*Cappon Magro*
Stewed Eels	*Anguille in Umido*
Fresh Tuna Bologna Style	*Il Tonno alla Bolognese*
Octopus, Squid, Cuttlefish	*Polipi, Seppie, Calamari*
Squid Neapolitan Style	*Sepie alla Napolenta*
Roast Fish	*Pesce Arrosto*
Poached Fish	*Pesce in Bianco*
Fried Prawns	*Gamberi Fritti*
Fried Scampi	*Scampi Fritti*
Mixed Fried Fish	*Fritto Misto di Mare*
Prawns with Ham	*Gamberi con Prosciutto alla griglia*
Oven-baked Mussels	*Cozze Gratinate*
Red Mullet Cooked in Paper Cases	*Triglie in Cartoccio*
Red Mullet Leghorn Style	*Triglie alla Livornese*
Sea Bass	*Spigola*
Baked Skate	*Razza al Forno*
Soles Venetian Style	*Sogliole all Veneziana*
Vicenza Salt Cod	*Baccalà alla Vicentina*
Lake Trout	*Trota dei Lago*

Fish

PESCE

꯫꯫꯫꯫꯫꯫꯫꯫꯫

The long, narrow Italian peninsula brings the whole country close to either the Mediterranean or the Adriatic. Even in the mountainous North, lake and river fish is plentiful and excellent. Wherever you go in Italy, you can eat really fresh fish. Much of it is quite different from ours. There are no Dover soles, hake or haddock, but in exchange there is red mullet (triglie) the 'woodcock of the sea', fresh tuna (tonnato), fresh sardines (sarde), and octopus, squid and cuttlefish (polipi, seppie, calamari).

Many of these warm-water fish are ugly, big-headed and bony, especially those which live in the rocks. The Italians do not waste them because of this; they make them into aromatic fish soups and stews. In this way, they extract all the flavour and goodness, and make the best of what flesh there is.

They name many by adding 'of the sea' (di mare) to whatever the creature looks like, and so there are sea dates (datteri di mare), small bivalves shaped like dates; they are cooked like mussels, which they resemble. There are also sea truffles (tartufi di mare), sea snails (lumache di mare) and many others.

Sea urchins or sea chestnuts (ricci) are purplish-black spiky balls which are cut in two and the iodine-strong orange interior is eaten raw or made into a sauce. I have seen them occasionally on sale in Soho.

The crawfish (aragosta), the spiky lobster with two antennae in place of pincers, is more usual than the lobster with claws. Scampi, a variation of the Dublin Bay prawn, is the 'in' dish now. (I have even heard tourists asking for it in Scandinavia, where the shrimps and freshwater crayfish are the best in the world.)

The Italians cook swordfish (pesce spada), which is like tuna in tex-

Fish

ture, but white; sturgeon (storione), our own royal fish; and fresh anchovies; as well as making full use of all the tiny fish they net.

John Dory (pesce San Pietro) used to be quite common in England, which leads to a sad tale. We could also buy brill, bream, saithe and monk fish, but now they are hard to find. We miss a lot by not taking full advantage of the fauna found round our coasts; and we throw away, or give to the cat, fish heads and bones instead of cooking them to make strong stocks for sauces, soups and stews. Many of the lesser-known fish have a better flavour and texture than the more popular ones.

One can buy quite a few Mediterranean fish in England, but when they are unobtainable we can use Italian recipes, both simple and urbane, to improve the fish we get from the fishmonger's slab or the deep-freeze. The Italians do fry fish, but their most distinctive seafood cookery is that in which they combine the vegetation of the land, such as tomatoes and herbs, with the yield of the sea.

Like all Catholic countries, Italy preserved fish for hundreds of years, before canning was invented. The Italians had dried cod, tuna in great barrels and other forms of preserved fish. Salt cod or stockfish is still eaten on Friday and fast days, especially in winter, and it can be cooked simply or with sophistication.

CRAWFISH FRA DIAVOLO AROGOSTA ALLA FRA DIAVOLO

The crawfish or spiny lobster is caught in the Mediterranean area, but our large-clawed lobsters can be used for this dish equally well.
4 small or 2 medium-sized boiled crawfish

For the Sauce

2 thinly-sliced onions
2 finely-chopped cloves of garlic
1 tablespoon olive oil
1 gill red wine
1 gill water
2 tablespoons tomato concentrate
pinch of cayenne (more, or less, according to taste)
plenty of freshly-ground black pepper
salt
1 tablespoon butter
1 dessertspoon flour

Fish

Cook the onion in hot oil until it softens and is translucent. Add the garlic and cook for 5 minutes. Add the wine, water, cayenne, pepper and salt. When it is hot stir in the tomato concentrate; cook for 15 minutes. Blend the butter and flour together until smooth, add it slowly to the sauce, stirring all the time, and cook until the sauce thickens.

Split the crawfish in halves lengthwise. Pour the sauce over. Put them in a hot oven (425°F) for 10 minutes. Serve at once.

SICILIAN COUSCOUS CUSCUSU ALLA SICILIANA

This dish is like the couscous from North Africa, but made with fish instead of mutton or chicken. The result is a glorified fish stew served with couscous (coarse semolina). As with all dishes of this kind, the more types of fish used the better, so make it for at least 6 people. In Sicily it is made in special pots which are like the Arabian 'keskes'. I used to bring couscous back from France, but I find it on sale in Greek and Cypriot shops now in England.

First prepare the Semolina

1 *lb. coarse semolina (couscous)*
1 *chopped onion*
1 *chopped clove of garlic*
pepper and salt
olive oil

1 *teaspoon cinnamon*
1 *teaspoon nutmeg*
½ *teaspoon ginger*
¼ *teaspoon powdered cloves*

Put the semolina in a large bowl, pour 2–3 tablespoons of hot water on it and stir it in with a fork. Leave to swell (about 20 minutes). Repeat this about three times; the grains should be swollen. Now rub the semolina between the fingers and thumbs to separate the grains. Season well with pepper and salt, and the spices, chopped onion and garlic. Steam it over hot water in a sieve or strainer, with a wet cloth between the saucepan and the strainer. Cover tightly to keep in the steam. Stir with a fork every so often.

Fish

For the Fish Stew

3–3½ lb. mixed firm-fleshed fish, including, if possible, lobster, scampi, prawns and conger eel
2 chopped onions
2 chopped cloves of garlic
3 tablespoons olive oil

pepper and salt
chopped parsley
chopped fresh basil, or dried basil
1 lb. peeled and quartered tomatoes
water

Fry the onion and garlic in oil till the onion softens. Add the fish cut into small pieces; cook for 2–3 minutes on each side. Just cover the fish with water, add pepper and salt, and the parsley, basil and tomatoes, and cook for 15–20 minutes or until the fish is cooked. Remove the fish, drain and keep warm. Put the couscous in a saucepan, add some of the fish stock, toss with a fork to separate the grains. Add some more fish stock. Serve on a dish with the fish on top and the rest of the fish stock as a sauce.

A FISH SALAD CAPPON MAGRO

This fish salad, sometimes called the Queen of Salads, is made in most seaside places in Italy, but it is traditionally Genoese. It really is a showy party piece. The greater the variety of vegetables and fish the more attractive and colourful it looks, and so it is best made for a number of people. It is built up on hard biscuits, or bread, like a pyramid.

Start the night before.

1. Take ½ lb. or more of hard biscuits (originally ship's issue biscuits were used for this dish), or 6–8 large slices of bread, crusts removed, crisped in the oven. Rub them with a crushed clove of garlic and marinate them overnight in olive oil and a little vinegar, in the proportion of three to one. There must be enough oil to impregnate the biscuits or bread thoroughly.

2. The next day boil about ½ lb. each of new potatoes, carrots, young green peas, French beans and sprigs of cauliflower. Do not overcook them as they must not be at all mushy. Slice the

Fish

potatoes, dice the carrots, cut up the French beans. Have also diced cooked beetroot, a small tin of sliced artichoke hearts, chopped celery, raw mushrooms marinated in olive oil, stoned black and green olives.

3. Prepare a mixture of shell-fish and white fish: ¾ pint of shelled prawns; a medium-sized freshly-boiled lobster, or tinned lobster; the meat from a medium-sized crab, or tinned crab; 6–7 scallops, removed from their shells and poached for 5 minutes; and 2 lb. poached firm white fish, such as turbot, halibut or cod. Remove the bones from the white fish and flake it. Cut up the lobster, if fresh lobster is used. Cut up the scallops, leaving fairly large pieces of the orange part. Season with oil, lemon juice, pepper and salt.

4. *For the Sauce*

1 tablespoon chopped parsley, 2 finely-chopped cloves of garlic, 3 chopped anchovy fillets, 1 tablespoon capers, 2 finely-chopped sweet-sour gherkins, 6 chopped stoned green olives, 4 hard-boiled-egg yolks, 1 tablespoon chopped pine nuts or walnuts, half a small heart of fennel (finocchio) finely chopped, a good handful of soft breadcrumbs soaked in a little milk and then the moisture squeezed out, about 1 gill of olive oil and 2 tablespoons wine vinegar.

Pound all the ingredients, except the oil and vinegar, in a mortar. Keep pounding until they are a soft mass. Gradually add the oil, stirring all the time with a wooden spoon, until the sauce is a thick cream, like stiff mayonnaise. Now gradually add the vinegar. The sauce must be thick enough to hold the vegetables and fish together.

5. *Decorations.*

12 cooked prawns in their shells, 3 sliced hard-boiled eggs, black and green olives, tinned anchovy fillets, tomato quarters.

6. Now the fun of constructing your pyramid begins.

Arrange the biscuits or bread on a large serving-dish. Put a layer of sauce on top, then a layer of mixed vegetables, a layer of fish and another layer of sauce. Continue in this way until you have used up all the ingredients. Decorate the salad with the prawns, eggs, olives, anchovies and tomato quarters. Serve really cold.

Fish

STEWED EELS ANGUILLE IN UMIDO

1½ lb. eel	1 gill white wine
1 sliced onion	1 gill water
¼ lb. sliced mushrooms	1 bay leaf
1 chopped clove of garlic	oil for frying
1 chopped carrot	chopped parsley
pepper and salt	

Get your fishmonger to skin the eels and cut them into 2-inch lengths. Fry the onion, garlic and carrot until they soften. Add the mushrooms; cook for 2 minutes. Add the eel; cover with the wine and water, season to taste, add the bay leaf. Cook gently for 30 minutes or until the fish is tender. Serve sprinkled with chopped parsley.

FRESH TUNA BOLOGNA STYLE IL TONNO ALLA BOLOGNESE

Fresh tuna is often available in Soho and specialist stores.

1½ lb. fresh tuna	2 chopped cloves of garlic
2 chopped onions	pepper and salt
2 chopped sticks of celery	1 gill dry white wine
2 chopped carrots	oil for frying

Fry the vegetables in hot oil until they soften. Add the fish; cover with the wine, add pepper and salt to taste. Simmer gently for about 30 minutes or until the fish is cooked. Serve cut in slices with the sauce poured over. If too much of the wine evaporates, add a little more.

OCTOPUS, SQUID, CUTTLEFISH POLIPI, SEPPIE, CALAMARI

I have often watched, fascinated, fishermen beating a fresh-caught octopus against a rock to make it tender. Quite a few fishmongers in England sell squid (seppie) and cuttlefish (calamari). These need long, slow cooking, especially if they are large. Tiny squid are fried crisp in Italy and they are most delicious, but if you want to eat them fried here, it is safer to boil them first as they are much larger.

SQUID NEAPOLITAN STYLE SEPPIE ALLA NAPOLENTA

Persuade your fishmonger to prepare the squid for you by cleaning it, removing the spine bone and the ink sacs and skinning it. Wash it well under running water. Cut the tentacles into strips and the body into narrow rings.

1–1¼ lb. squid
2 chopped cloves of garlic
2 sliced onions
1 lb. skinned, chopped tomatoes, or a medium-sized tin
1 tablespoon sultanas
12 chopped stoned black olives
pepper and salt
1 gill water
3 tablespoons olive oil

Brown the garlic and onions in the hot oil. Add the pieces of squid; let them brown. Add the tomatoes, sultanas, olives, pepper and salt to taste, and the water. Cover and cook gently until the squid is tender (about 1½–2 hours). Serve with plain boiled rice.

ROAST FISH PESCE ARROSTO

Use whole fish; whiting, fresh haddock, sea bass, sea bream or a small cod are suitable.

2–2½ lb. fish
olive oil
pepper and salt
chopped fresh marjoram or parsley

Score the fish three times on both sides. Brush it over with olive oil. Sprinkle with pepper, salt and chopped marjoram or parsley. Put it on a grid in a baking-tin and cook in a hot oven (425°F) for 20–25 minutes, depending on the thickness of the fish. Baste now and again with oil. Serve sprinkled with more chopped fresh marjoram or parsley.

Fish

POACHED FISH PESCE IN BIANCO

2–2½ lb. fish
pepper and salt
1 bay leaf
1 small chopped onion

Put the fish in a large pan or fish kettle, cover with cold water, add the pepper, salt, onion and bay leaf. Bring slowly to the boil. Let it cook gently for 15–20 minutes. The time will depend on the type and size of fish. Drain well. Serve sprinkled with lemon juice.

FRIED PRAWNS GAMBERI FRITTI

1 lb. cooked, shelled large prawns
oil for frying
1 pint frying-batter (pastella) (see page 112)

Dip the prawns in the batter and fry a few at a time in fairly deep oil. Drain well. Serve plain with lemon juice or with tomato or green sauce (see pages 150 and 151).

FRIED SCAMPI SCAMPI FRITTI

Choose deep-frozen or fresh scampi or Dublin Bay prawns.

16–24 scampi
frying-batter (pastella) (see page 112)
  or flour, egg and breadcrumbs
  for coating
oil for frying
lemon wedges

Put the scampi in hot water; bring it to the boil, then simmer for 1 minute. Remove the scampi, drain, and remove the shells. Dip in frying-batter or coat with flour, egg and breadcrumbs. Fry in deep oil, a few at a time. Serve with wedges of lemon.

MIXED FRIED FISH FRITTO MISTO DI MARE

2 lb. small pieces of fish, including
  prawns
frying-batter (pastella) (see page 112)
oil for frying
lemon wedges

Fish

Use as many different kinds of fish as possible. Cut them into small pieces, dip in batter and fry a few at a time in hot oil. Serve with lemon wedges.

PRAWNS WITH HAM GAMBERI CON PROSCIUTTO ALLA GRIGLIA

20–24 *cooked, shelled large prawns*
20–24 *thin slices of prosciutto (raw ham) or cooked ham*
pepper

egg and fine brown breadcrumbs for coating
lemon wedges

Season the prawns with pepper. Wrap each one in a slice of ham, securing with cotton. Stick 5–6 of them on small skewers. Dip in egg and breadcrumbs and grill gently until lightly browned. Serve with lemon wedges.

OVEN-BAKED MUSSELS COZZE GRATINATE

In Taranto they make a simple dish of mussels, very like the classic French dish of snails with garlic butter.

2 quarts cleaned and bearded mussels
finely-chopped cloves of garlic (at least 2 cloves)

2 tablespoons olive oil
chopped parsley or marjoram
brown breadcrumbs
pepper and salt

Open the mussels, with an oyster knife if you have one, or by heating them in the oven until they open. Remove half the shell, leaving each mussel in its half-shell. Arrange them in a fireproof dish. Pound the garlic, oil, herbs, pepper and salt together until smooth. Put a little of this mixture on each mussel; top with breadcrumbs. Brown in a medium-hot oven (380°F–400°F). Serve as an entrée or as a hot antipasti.

Fish

RED MULLET COOKED IN PAPER CASES TRIGLIE IN CARTOCCIO

4 medium-sized red mullet
1 finely-chopped onion
1 finely-chopped clove of garlic
1 chopped celery stalk
olive oil for frying

chopped fresh basil or parsley
½ teaspoon pepper
½ teaspoon salt
1 teaspoon ginger

Soften the onion and garlic in the hot oil. Add the celery, basil or parsley, pepper, salt and ginger and mix together. Make 2 incisions on each side of the fish; sprinkle the onion mixture on top; wrap each fish separately in greased greaseproof paper or aluminium foil. Bake in a moderate oven (375°F) for 30–35 minutes or until the fish is cooked. Serve each fish in its little packet so that none of the sauce is lost.

RED MULLET LEGHORN STYLE TRIGLIE ALLA LIVORNESE

Allow 1 or 2 red mullet, according to size, per person. Wipe them, scale but do not clean them; they have a much better flavour this way.

red mullet
1 small chopped onion
1 chopped, crushed clove of garlic
1 chopped stick of celery

1 lb. skinned, chopped tomatoes
pepper and salt
chopped parsley
oil for frying

Fry the onion, garlic and celery in hot oil until they begin to brown. Add the tomatoes, pepper and salt. Cook until the tomatoes are really soft. Rub the vegetables through a fine sieve, or put them through a vegetable mill. Put the fish in a pan, cover with the purée, add the chopped parsley and cook for 5–10 minutes, according to the size of the fish.

SEA BASS SPIGOLA

Sea bass is often on sale in Soho and many fishmongers in different parts of London. It is a delicately flavoured, most delicious fish.

Fish

2½–3 lb. sea bass
dried fennel sticks

oil
lemon slices

Remove the scales and clean the fish. Score it two or three times on both sides. Sprinkle it with oil, lay the fennel sticks on top and grill slowly on both sides until it is cooked. Serve with slices of lemon.

BAKED SKATE RAZZA AL FORNO

1½–1¾ lb. skate cut in pieces
1 chopped onion
2 chopped cloves of garlic
3 chopped anchovy fillets
1 tablespoon capers

pepper
chopped parsley
olive oil
lemon juice

Arrange the fish in a fireproof dish. Soften the onion and garlic in hot oil; add the anchovies, capers and pepper; stir to mix; pour the mixture over the fish. Sprinkle plentifully with olive oil and a little lemon juice. Bake in a moderately hot oven (380°F) for about 30 minutes or until the fish is cooked.

SOLES VENETIAN STYLE SOGLIOLE ALLA VENEZIANA

4 medium-sized soles, skinned on both sides
flour for coating
1 finely-chopped onion
2 tablespoons sultanas

2 tablespoons pine nuts
butter for frying
1 gill white wine vinegar
1 gill water
pepper and salt

Coat the soles with flour. Heat the butter; add the sultanas, pine nuts and soles. Fry the soles until they are brown on both sides and cooked. Keep them hot. Fry the onion until it softens and colours slightly; add the vinegar and water, with pepper and salt to taste; cook for 10 minutes. Serve the soles with the sauce poured over.

Fish

VICENZA SALT COD BACCALÀ ALLA VICENTINA

1½ lb. salt cod
3 finely-chopped onions
2 chopped cloves of garlic
olive oil

hot milk
freshly-ground black pepper
½ teaspoon cinnamon
½ teaspoon ginger

Soak the cod for 24 hours, changing the water 3–4 times. Fry the onions in hot oil until they soften. Add the garlic; cook for 5 minutes. Add the fish and plenty of hot milk. Add the pepper and spices. Cover the saucepan and simmer very slowly until the fish is tender (at least 2 hours). Add more milk if necessary. Correct the seasoning; it may need a little salt. In the traditional recipe pounded anchovies are added, but I think this makes the dish far too salt. This dish is usually served with boiled or fried polenta (see page 66).

LAKE TROUT TROTA DEI LAGO

Italian trout are exceptionally good. They are usually served very simply—poached, fried or grilled. Allow 1 trout per person.

4 trout
2 tablespoons chopped parsley
lemon wedges

salt
butter for frying

Clean, wash and dry the trout. Heat the butter and fry the fish on both sides until it is golden-brown. Serve sprinkled with salt and chopped parsley, with lemon wedges. Boiled new potatoes go well.

Meat

LE CARNE

Italian Boiled Dinner	*Bollito*
Florentine Steak	*Costata alla Fiorentina*
Steak with Tomato and Garlic Sauce	*Bistecca alla Pizzaiola*
Meat Balls	*Polpette*
Beef Stew with Cloves	*Il Garofalata*
Bolognese Beef Stew	*Stufato di Manzo alla Bolognese*
Goulash	*Goulash*
Stewed Lamb	*Stufato di Agnello*
Lamb Chops Milan Style	*Costolette di Agnello alla Milanese*
Roast Lamb	*Agnello Arrosto*
Roast Baby Lamb	*Abbacchio al Forno*
Stewed Lamb's Offal	*Coratella di Agnello*
Lamb's Tongues with Oranges	*Lingue di Agnello all' Agrigento*
Pork with Orange	*Maiale Con Arancia*
Pork Chops with Fennel	*Costa di Maiale con Finocchio*
Pork Stewed in Milk Bologna Style	*Maiale al Latte alla Bolognese*
Florentine Roast Pork	*Arrosto di Maiale alla Fiorentina*
Perugian Roast Pork	*Arrosto di Maiale alla Perugina*
Calf's Tongues	*Lingue di Vitello*
Calf's Liver with Parmesan Cheese	*Fegato di Vitello al Parmigiana*
Stewed Kidneys with White Wine	*Rognoni con Vino Bianco*

Meat

Kidneys with Marsala	*Rognoni al Marsala*
Mixed Fry	*Fritto Misto*
Frying-batter	*Pastella*
Skewered Mixed Fry	*Fritto alla Stecco*
Baked Tripe	*Trippa al Forno*
Stewed Tripe	*Trippa Stufato*
Veal Chops with Mushrooms	*Braciole di Vitello con Funghi*
Veal Cutlets	*Costolette di Vitello*
Breaded Veal Cutlets Milan Style	*Cotolette di Vitella alla Milanese*
Veal Escalopes	*Scaloppe di Vitello*
Veal with Zabaglione	*Vitello allo Zabaglione*
Veal with Tuna Fish Sauce	*Vitello Tonnato*
Tuna Fish Sauce	*Tonnato*
Veal Stew	*Stufato di Vitello*
Sicilian Stewed Veal	*Vitello alla Siciliana*
Hollow Bone Stew	*Osso Bucco*
Saltimbocca	*Saltimbocca*
Bocconcini	*Bocconcini*
Farsumagru	*Farsumagru*
Genoese Stuffed Veal	*Cima alla Genovese*
Stuffed Veal Rolls	*Messicani*

Meat

LE CARNE

After the antipasti and the pasta or soup, the Italians come to the meat. They approach this course with discrimination, cooking it to get the maximum enjoyment out of the quality of the meat they are using, and—in spite of toutist criticism—Italian meat can be first-rate.

Veal comes in three 'sizes'. Vitello di latte is killed while the calf is still entirely milk-fed; the flesh is white and delicate. Vitello is more like our home-killed veal and the calf is up to six or nine months old. Vitellone is really baby beef and is inclined to be neither one thing nor the other. Beef varies from the splendid, to cuts from oxen which have worked in the fields, when it is only fit for slow stewing.

Abbacchio is baby lamb; a whole one is just about enough for 5–6 people. Then there is agnello which is like our spring lamb. It is not 'done' to eat mutton, except perhaps cooked in a stew or disguised as venison.

Pork ranges from the sucking pig (porchetta) to the fattened porker (maiale).

The Italians also eat kid, goat and venison, and the chamois and wild boar of the mountains.

The grills and roasts are mainly plain, with perhaps a few herbs to give extra flavour. Stews have vegetables, tomatoes, cloves, rosemary, basil, oregano, juniper berries and many other herbs and spices added to them. Many dishes are cooked Hunter Style (cacciatora), which means that they are simple and uncomplicated and easily cooked on a camp fire.

The Italians mince quite a lot of their meat. Their meat-balls (polpette) are excellent, often combining two or more meats.

Meat

They use minced meat to give body to their ragù (meat sauce).

ITALIAN BOILED DINNER BOLLITO

This famous stew from Piedmont in the North is like the large stews from many parts of the world—for instance, the Cucido or Sancocho of the West Indies and to a lesser degree the Pot-au-feu of France. It is not to be made for a small family, because it must have different kinds of meat, including chicken as well as veal, beef, boiled sausage (cotechino), calf's head and calf's foot. The meat is cooked in a large pot, the piece that takes the longest to cook being put in first. It is served with haricot beans, potatoes and cabbage; and a green sauce (salsa verde) (see page 150), or a tomato sauce (see pages 151, 152), goes with it. It can be made for fewer people by leaving out some of the meat and using smaller cuts. I like to cook the vegetables, too, in it as it makes such a tasty broth. It can also be eaten cold, if there is any left over. It sounds a homely dish, but it is only homely in the sense of it being a family dish, for its flavour is regal.

1 *boiling-fowl*
1 *knuckle of veal*
2–2½ *lb. lean beef (chuck or topside)*
cotechino (see page 27)
1 *calf's foot*
1 *lb. haricot beans soaked overnight*

1 *cabbage cut in quarters*
potatoes
water
1 *dessertspoon salt*
freshly-ground black pepper

Fill a large saucepan with water and bring it to the boil. Cook the calf's foot and the knuckle of veal for 45 minutes, then add the fowl and the beef; they will take from 2–2½ hours according to size and cut. Add the beans and the cotechino (or, failing this, smoked sausage). Simmer gently for 1 hour, then add the salt and pepper. Add the peeled potatoes and cook them whole for about 40–45 minutes. Lastly, add the cabbage. Cook gently until all the meats

Meat

are cooked. Put slices of meat and pieces of chicken on a large dish, arrange the vegetables round them and serve the sauce separately. The broth makes an excellent soup.

FLORENTINE STEAK COSTATA ALLA FIORENTINA

The true Florentine steak weighs at least one pound, and it should be from the wonderful local cattle which have grazed on the lush pastures of the Chiana Valley. It is cut in a special way, from the ribs, in and near Florence and Siena. It is the best steak in Italy. A good red Chianti should be drunk with it. It is grilled over charcoal and seasoned with salt and pepper after it is cooked. If salt is sprinkled on before cooking, the juices will run.

If you suspect that your steak may not be as tender as it should be, you can marinade it before cooking.

Porterhouse or T-bone steak cut   pepper and salt
*   really thick   lemon juice*
olive oil   lemon wedges

Mix the olive oil, pepper, salt and a little lemon juice together. Marinate the steak in this for an hour, turning it over occasionally. It should be grilled over charcoal; failing that, get the griller really hot. Grill it for 4–5 minutes on each side, longer if you do not want it rare, but it should not be overcooked. Serve with lemon wedges.

STEAK WITH TOMATO AND GARLIC SAUCE BISTECCA ALLA PIZZAIOLA

This is a good way of cooking less fine cuts of steak. Rump or fillet skirt would do very well.

1½ lb. fillet or rump skirt   chopped fresh basil or parsley
2 lb. peeled and quartered tomatoes   pepper and salt
4 chopped cloves of garlic   oil

Beat the steak well. Cook the tomatoes, garlic and basil or parsley,

Meat

in a little oil. Season to taste. Simmer for 30 minutes. Brown the meat on both sides, add it to the sauce and cook for 8–10 minutes. Serve the meat and the sauce together.

MEAT BALLS POLPETTE

These are much nicer when made with uncooked minced meat. It can be veal, beef or pork or a mixture of all three.

1½ lb. minced meat	1 tablespoon finely-chopped parsley
1 thick slice of bread, soaked in milk	2 eggs
1 minced clove of garlic	pepper and salt

Squeeze the moisture from the bread, then mix the bread, meat, garlic, parsley, eggs and pepper and salt. Beat well together. Shape into small balls or little flat cakes. Fry on both sides in hot butter until they are brown (about 7–8 minutes). Serve with a salad or with a tomato sauce (see pages 151, 152).

BEEF STEW WITH CLOVES IL GAROFOLATA

1½–2 lb. topside, or chuck steak, in 1 piece	beef stock
strips of fat bacon for larding	6 cloves
1 chopped onion	¼ teaspoon ground ginger
2 chopped cloves of garlic	¼ teaspoon nutmeg
1 lb. skinned and quartered tomatoes	pepper and salt
1 gill red wine	olive oil or fat for frying
	1 tablespoon chopped marjoram or parsley

Lard the meat with strips of fat bacon. Heat the oil in a heavy saucepan and brown the meat all over. Add the vegetables, wine and enough stock just to cover the meat, then add the spices, pepper and salt. Simmer gently for 2–2½ hours or until the meat is tender. Serve sliced, with potato gnocchi (see page 63).

Meat

BOLOGNESE BEEF STEW STUFATO DI MANZO ALLA BOLOGNESE

1 lb. lean stewing-beef (chuck or skirt)
¼ lb. lean ham or gammon rashers
¼ lb. chicken livers
1 large chopped onion
1 chopped clove of garlic
3–4 chopped sticks of celery
¼ lb. sliced mushrooms
1 tablespoon tomato concentrate
pepper and salt
butter for frying
½ pint hot water

Dice the meat and ham. Cut up the chicken livers. Heat the butter, add the meat, ham and livers and cook for 5 minutes. Add the vegetables and mushrooms; stir and fry for 5 minutes. Add the hot water, pepper and salt, and stir in the tomato concentrate. Cook slowly for 2–2½ hours until the meat is tender.

GOULASH

Although goulash originated in Hungary, it has been made in and around Trieste for many years and has become one of their specialities

1½–2 lb. stewing-steak cut into small chunks
4 chopped onions
2 chopped cloves of garlic
2 lb. skinned and quartered tomatoes
pepper and salt
bay leaf
1 tablespoon paprika
pinch of ginger
a little flour
oil for frying

Lightly flour the meat and fry it in hot oil until brown all over. Brown the onions and garlic until lightly brown. Cook the meat, onions, garlic and tomatoes together; season with the pepper, salt, bay leaf, ginger and paprika; press the tomatoes to extract all the juice. Stew slowly for 2–2½ hours. The sauce should be very thick. Correct the seasoning and serve with plain boiled spaghetti.

Meat

STEWED LAMB STUFATO DI AGNELLO

1½–2 lb. stewing-lamb cut in
    bite-sized pieces
2 chopped onions
2 chopped carrots
2 chopped cloves of garlic
2 large peeled and quartered potatoes
1 chopped stalk of celery
1 bay leaf
4–6 oz. shelled green peas
1 teaspoon powdered rosemary
pepper and salt
1 gill dry white wine
1 pint water
seasoned flour
fat for frying

Coat the meat with the seasoned flour and brown it in the hot fat. Add the vegetables, herbs, pepper, salt, wine and water. Simmer gently until the meat is tender (about 1–1½ hours). Correct the seasoning.

LAMB CHOPS MILAN STYLE COSTOLETTE DI AGNELLO ALLA MILANESE

4 lamb chops
1 beaten egg
fine brown breadcrumbs
grated cheese
pepper and salt
olive oil

Mix together equal quantities of breadcrumbs and grated cheese; add pepper and salt to taste. Dip the chops in the beaten egg, then in the breadcrumbs and cheese. Sprinkle with olive oil. Grill on both sides for 5–10 minutes, according to how well done you like them.

ROAST LAMB AGNELLO ARROSTO

½ leg of lamb, or 1 small leg
2 cloves of garlic
rosemary
1 gill dry white wine

Make 2 slits in the leg of lamb and stick in the peeled and crushed cloves of garlic and a spike or two of rosemary. Cook in a hot oven (425°F–450°F), allowing 15 minutes per pound and 15 minutes over. When the lamb has been cooking for 15 minutes, pour the wine over. Baste it once or twice whilst it is cooking. Make a gravy with the pan juices.

ROAST BABY LAMB ABBACCHIO AL FORNO

This is a Roman speciality. The baby lamb is quite different in flavour from the spring lamb usually bought in England, but occasionally one can get it. It is usually served well cooked.

1 *small leg of very young lamb*
1 *crushed clove of garlic*
pepper and salt
a sprig of rosemary, or powdered rosemary

Put the crushed clove of garlic near the shank end. Season well with pepper and salt, add the rosemary. Roast the meat in a hot oven (425°F–450°F) until the meat is well done and really crisp outside.

STEWED LAMB'S OFFAL CORATELLA DI AGNELLO

There are no unpopular parts of a beast in countries where meat can be scarce and expensive. Imagination, cunning and skill are used to make excellent dishes from parts we consider inedible, from lungs to mountain oysters (testicoli).

1 *lamb's heart*
½ *lb. lamb's liver*
2 *soaked and blanched lamb's tongues*
1 *chopped onion*
1 *chopped clove of garlic*
1 *tablespoon chopped parsley*
1 *medium-sized tin of artichoke hearts*
juice of ½ lemon
1 *gill red wine*
2 *chopped anchovies*
fat for frying
pepper and salt

Slice the heart, liver and tongues thinly. Cook the tongues in hot fat for 2–3 minutes. Add the heart; cook for 5 minutes. Add the onion and garlic; cook for 15 minutes. Add the liver; cook for 5 minutes. Add the wine, anchovies and artichokes, and pepper and salt to taste. Simmer gently for 10–15 minutes or until the tongue and heart are tender. Add the chopped parsley and lemon juice.

Serve hot. If liked, the lungs (lights) and the spleen (melts) can be used, as they are in Italy.

LAMB'S TONGUES WITH ORANGES LINGUE DI AGNELLO ALL'AGRIGENTO

Here fruit is cooked with meat; this goes back to Roman times. I can never understand why many foreigners are so surprised at our English red currant jelly with roast mutton or gooseberry sauce with mackerel, when they have so many 'sweet and sour' combinations.

8 lamb's tongues
2–3 oranges, according to size
butter
3 tablespoons tomato concentrate
pepper and salt
juice of 1 large orange

Cook the tongues in boiling salted water until they are tender (1–1½ hours). Peel and quarter the oranges, taking care to remove all pith. Remove the tongues from the water and skin them; dry thoroughly. Heat the butter, but do not let it brown, and fry the tongues until they are brown all over. Reduce the heat, add the orange juice and when it is hot, stir in the tomato concentrate. Season to taste. Add the orange quarters; let them heat through. Serve hot.

PORK WITH ORANGE MAIALE CON ARANCIA

4 pork chops
grated rind and juice of 1 orange
slices of orange
1 large chopped clove of garlic
rosemary
pepper and salt
2 tablespoons Marsala or sherry

Make an incision in each chop and put a small piece of garlic and a leaf or two of rosemary in each of them. Sprinkle with orange rind, pepper and salt. Mix the orange juice and the Marsala or sherry together, pour this over the chops and let them marinate for about an hour. Remove the chops, pat them dry and brown them on both sides under the griller or in a frying-pan. Arrange the orange slices in a fireproof dish, put the chops on top, add the marinade and finish cooking the chops in a moderate oven (350°F–375°F) for 20–25 minutes.

PORK CHOPS WITH FENNEL COSTA DI MAIALE CON FINOCCHIO

4 pork chops
fat for frying
1 gill dry red wine
2 tablespoons Marsala
1 crushed clove of garlic
1 tablespoon tomato concentrate
½ teaspoon fennel seeds
pepper and salt

Brown the chops in hot fat on both sides, then continue cooking slowly for 25 minutes, turning frequently. Keep them hot. Brown the clove of garlic in the pan, add the wine, pepper and salt, tomato concentrate and fennel seeds. Cook briskly for 6–7 minutes. Strain the sauce over the chops and serve at once.

PORK STEWED IN MILK BOLOGNA STYLE MAIALE AL LATTE ALLA BOLOGNESE

1–1½ lb. boned lean loin of pork
1 chopped onion
1 chopped clove of garlic
2 chopped rashers of streaky bacon
pepper and salt
fat for frying
1–1¼ pints milk
1 teaspoon coriander seeds

If the pork is fat, remove some of the fat. Sprinkle the meat with pepper and salt and leave for 2 hours. Cover the inside of the meat with garlic and coriander seeds, then roll the meat and tie it with string. Fry the onion and chopped bacon in the fat until the onion has softened. Brown the meat on all sides. Transfer the meat, onion and bacon into a saucepan just large enough to take the meat. Heat the milk and pour it over; cover the pan tightly; simmer very gently for 1½ hours. Uncover the pan and cook for a further 30 minutes. The milk will reduce considerably. If necessary, add a little more hot milk to prevent burning. The sauce will become golden-brown. The pork can be served hot with the sauce, or it is equally delicious if allowed to cool in the sauce and served cold.

FLORENTINE ROAST PORK ARROSTO DI MAIALE ALLA FIORENTINA

3–3½ lb. loin of pork
3 cloves of garlic
a few sprigs of rosemary
6 cloves
pepper and salt
1 pint of water

Cut the garlic into slices. Insert them here and there in the joint of pork, tuck in two or three sprigs of rosemary and stud with the cloves. Season with pepper and salt. Put the water in the baking-pan. Bake the meat in a moderately hot oven (420°F) for 2¼–2½ hours, about 45 minutes per lb. The meat remains juicy. Serve it hot or cold.

PERUGIAN ROAST PORK ARROSTO DI MAIALE ALLA PERUGINA

This is cooked in the same way as Florentine Roast Pork (see above) but it is flavoured with fennel (leaves or seeds) and garlic.

CALF'S TONGUES LINGUE DI VITELLO

2–3 calf's tongues
1 finely-chopped onion
1 finely-chopped carrot
1 finely-chopped clove of garlic
1 finely-chopped celery stalk
4 oz. sliced mushrooms
1 tablespoon tomato concentrate
3 tablespoons sweet white wine
juice of 1 lemon
pepper and salt
oil for frying
chopped parsley

Cook the tongues in boiling salted water for about 1 hour or until they are tender. Skin them. This is best done by plunging them into cold water for a few minutes, then remove them, make a

Meat

nick at the base of the tongue and gently pull off the skin. Cut the tongues into slices. Fry the onion, carrot, garlic, celery and mushrooms in hot oil until they have softened. Add the slices of tongue; cook them, turning frequently, for 5-6 minutes. Add the wine, lemon juice, pepper and salt. Dissolve the tomato concentrate in a little of the sauce when it is hot; cook for 5 minutes. Serve the tongues covered with the sauce and sprinkled with chopped parsley. This dish can be made with an ox tongue, but the cooking time will be much longer (30 minutes per pound and 30 minutes over) and it will then feed up to twelve people.

CALF'S LIVER WITH PARMESAN CHEESE FEGATO DI VITELLO AL PARMIGIANA

1 lb. calf's liver cut in ¼-inch slices
2 large chopped onions
1 chopped clove of garlic
¼ teaspoon dried marjoram

pepper and salt
olive oil
grated Parmesan cheese
fine brown breadcrumbs

Cook the onions and garlic in olive oil until they are softened and turn golden. Brown the liver quickly on both sides to seal in the juices. Cover the liver with the onions and garlic, the marjoram, and pepper and salt to taste. Mix plenty of grated Parmesan cheese with the breadcrumbs and sprinkle on top. Put the frying-pan under a hot grill and cook until the top is nicely browned.

STEWED KIDNEYS WITH WHITE WINE ROGNONI CON VINO BIANCO

1 lb. veal kidneys
pepper and salt
butter for frying

1 glass white wine
lemon juice
2 finely-sliced onions

Remove the fat and skin from the kidneys, cut out the hard core, wash them well. Slice them in halves and slice each half into small pieces; season with pepper and salt. Fry the onions in hot butter

Meat

until they soften, then add the kidneys and cook them for 2–3 minutes. Add the wine and a little lemon juice; simmer very gently for 20–30 minutes. If necessary, add a little more wine or stock.

KIDNEYS WITH MARSALA ROGNONI AL MARSALA

1 lb. veal kidneys
2 finely-sliced onions
2 finely-chopped cloves of garlic
½ lb. sliced mushrooms

pepper and salt
butter for frying
4 tablespoons Marsala or sherry

Prepare the kidneys as shown on previous page. Fry the onions and garlic in hot butter. Add the kidneys; let them brown. Add the mushrooms; cook for 3–4 minutes. Season to taste. Cook very slowly for 15 minutes, then add the Marsala or sherry and continue to cook slowly for 15 minutes longer.

MIXED FRY FRITTO MISTO

This can be a mixture of sweetbreads, brains, liver, small slices of veal, mushrooms, small pieces of cauliflower and artichoke hearts. You can have a mixture of several ingredients or just a few. Ideally all the ingredients should be cooked separately as they will take different times to cook. They can be dipped in frying-batter (pastella, see the next recipe) or in egg and breadcrumbs before frying.

SWEETBREADS ANIMELLE
Soak the sweetbreads in salted water for an hour. Blanch them in boiling water for a few minutes, then plunge them into cold water. Remove the skin and cut them into slices about 1 inch thick. Dip them in beaten egg, coat with fine brown breadcrumbs and fry in hot butter until golden.

BRAINS CERVELLO
Soak the brains in cold water for 30 minutes. Blanch them for 2 minutes, drain well, remove the skin. Cut them into small pieces.

Meat

Dip them in beaten egg, coat with breadcrumbs and fry in hot butter until golden.

Calf's Liver FEGATO
Cut the liver into small slices, dip them in flour and fry in hot butter, about 3–4 minutes each side.

Veal VITELLO
Flatten some small thin pieces of tender veal, season them with pepper and salt, dredge lightly with flour. Fry in hot butter until brown on both sides.

Mushrooms FUNGHI
Choose fairly large, firm mushrooms. Cut them into ¼-inch-thick slices including the stalks. Fry them in hot butter or oil until they are tender and light brown.

Cauliflower CAVOLFIORE
Wash the cauliflower and break it into flowerets. Cook it in boiling salted water for 15 minutes. Drain well. Coat with egg and breadcrumbs and fry until golden.

Artichokes CARCIOFI
If using tinned ones, drain them well, coat with egg and breadcrumbs and fry until golden. Fresh ones should be cooked in boiling salted water until nearly tender, then drained; the leaves and choke should be removed and the hearts coated, then fried.

FRYING-BATTER PASTELLA

If preferred, the ingredients for the Fritto Misto may be dipped in a frying-batter before being cooked.

4 oz. flour
a good pinch of salt
2–3 tablespoons olive oil
lukewarm water
1 stiffly-beaten egg white

Meat

This should be made at least 1 hour before using. Sift the flour and salt together, then gradually add enough olive oil and enough lukewarm water to make a thin cream. Just before using the batter, gently fold in the egg white.

SKEWERED MIXED FRY FRITTO ALLO STECCO

small squares of veal cut thin
sweetbreads, washed, blanched and cut in small pieces
brains, washed, blanched and cut in small pieces
mushroom caps
beaten egg yolk
fine brown breadcrumbs
pepper and salt
oil for frying

Arrange the meat and mushroom caps on skewers. Season to taste. Dip them in the egg and breadcrumbs. Fry in hot oil until brown and crisp.

BAKED TRIPE TRIPPA AL FORNO

1½–1¾ lb. prepared tripe
1 large finely-chopped onion
1 chopped clove of garlic
1 chopped carrot
¼ lb. sliced mushrooms
2 chopped celery stalks
2 tablespoons tomato concentrate
1 bay leaf
pepper and salt
1 pint water
grated Parmesan cheese
oil for frying

Cut the tripe into strips about ½ inch wide and 2 inches long. Cook it in boiling salted water for 1 hour. Drain well. Fry the onion, garlic, carrot and celery in hot oil until they brown. Add the mushrooms, water, pepper, salt and bay leaf; stir in the tomato concentrate when the water is hot. Add the tripe and bake in a moderate oven (350°F–375°F) for 1 hour. Cook covered for the first 30 minutes, then add grated Parmesan cheese and finish the cooking without a lid.

Meat

STEWED TRIPE TRIPPA STUFATO

1½–1¾ lb. prepared tripe
1 pint water
2 chopped onions
2 chopped carrots
2 chopped celery stalks

1 tablespoon brown sugar
1 teaspoon made mustard
pepper and salt
1 tablespoon flour diluted with a
    little cold water

Cut the tripe into squares, put it in a heavy saucepan, just cover with water, add the onions, carrots, celery, sugar, mustard, pepper and salt. Bring to the boil, then simmer gently until the tripe is tender (2–2½ hours). Add the diluted flour, stirring until it thickens, and cook for 15 minutes. Correct the seasoning.

VEAL CHOPS WITH MUSHROOMS BRACIOLE DI VITELLO CON FUNGHI

4 veal chops
2 sliced carrots
1 chopped onion
½ lb. peeled, chopped tomatoes

¼ lb. sliced mushrooms
pepper and salt
1 gill dry white wine
olive oil for frying

Brown the chops on both sides in the hot oil. Add the carrots, onion and mushrooms; let them cook and soften. Add the tomatoes, wine and pepper and salt. Cover and simmer gently for 1 hour. Turn the chops once or twice. If necessary, add a little more wine or veal stock so that the chops are kept moist.

VEAL CUTLETS COSTOLETTE DI VITELLO

8 veal cutlets
1 large sliced onion
1 chopped clove of garlic
1 small tin of tomatoes
¼ lb. sliced mushrooms

1 gill red wine
pepper and salt
2 tablespoons tomato concentrate
oil for frying

Brown the cutlets in hot oil. Add the onions and garlic and cook until the onions are transparent. Add the tinned tomatoes, mush-

Meat

rooms, wine, pepper and salt to taste. When all is hot, mix in the tomato concentrate. Simmer gently for 40–50 minutes.

BREADED VEAL CUTLETS MILAN STYLE COTOLETTE DI VITELLO ALLA MILANESE

8 *veal cutlets*
flour, egg and breadcrumbs for coating
2 *chopped cloves of garlic*
chopped parsley
pepper and salt
lemon slices
oil for frying

Season the cutlets and coat them with flour, egg and breadcrumbs. Fry them in hot oil until golden-brown on both sides, then reduce the heat and cook them slowly for 20 minutes, turning them once or twice. Serve sprinkled with chopped parsley and slices of lemon.

VEAL ESCALOPES SCALOPPE DI VITELLO

4 *thin slices of veal cut from the fillet*
1 *chopped clove of garlic*
½ *lb. skinned and quartered tomatoes*
¼ *lb. sliced mushrooms*
pepper and salt
1 *gill dry white wine*
oil for frying
grated Parmesan cheese

Heat the oil and garlic together. Add the meat and brown it on both sides. Add the tomatoes, mushrooms, wine, pepper and salt. Simmer gently for 20 minutes. Serve sprinkled with Parmesan cheese.

VEAL WITH ZABAGLIONE VITELLO ALLO ZABAGLIONE

4 *thin slices of veal cut from the fillet or leg*
4 *slices of bread*
seasoned flour
butter for frying

Fry the bread in hot butter until golden brown. Keep it hot. Put the flour in a bag and shake the slices of veal in it until they are lightly covered. Cook them in butter until brown on both sides. Keep them hot while you make the sauce.

Meat

For the Sauce

2 tablespoons Marsala or sherry
1 dessertspoon lemon juice
1 tablespoon water

2 beaten egg yolks
pepper and salt

Pour the Marsala or sherry, with the lemon juice and water, into the pan the meat was cooked in. Add pepper and salt to taste, stir and let it cook for 1 minute. Let it cool a little, then pour it slowly on to the egg yolks, stirring gently. Put the basin over hot water and beat until the sauce is light and frothy and has thickened.

VEAL WITH TUNA FISH SAUCE VITELLO TONNATO

This is, I think, one of the most delicious cold meat dishes. I first ate it in San Remo; it was strongly recommended by the Patron, who graciously offered us a bottle of Asti Spumante as we were the first customers that day. This is his recipe.

2 lb. leg of veal, bone removed
1 chopped carrot
1 chopped onion
1 chopped celery stalk

1 bay leaf
3–4 peppercorns
salt to taste
boiling water

Tie the meat up into a neat shape. Just cover it with boiling water. Add the vegetables, bay leaf, salt and peppercorns. Simmer gently for 1½–2 hours until the meat is tender. Remove the meat, let it cool, then slice it thinly. Arrange the slices, overlapping, in a deep dish. Cover with tuna fish sauce (see below). Leave it in a cool place a day or two before serving.

TUNA FISH SAUCE TONNATO

1 4-oz. tin best-quality tuna fish in oil
3–4 anchovy fillets
olive oil

2 tablespoons capers drained free of vinegar
lemon juice
pepper

Pound the tuna fish and anchovy fillets in a mortar or basin and add enough oil to make a thin mayonnaise. Stir the oil in slowly. Add lemon juice to taste, add the capers and pepper. Stir to mix, correct the seasoning.

VEAL STEW STUFATO DI VITELLO

1½–2 lb. breast of veal
3 chopped cloves of garlic
1 sprig of rosemary
1 medium-sized tin of tomatoes
1 gill white wine
pepper and salt
oil for frying

Trim the meat and cut it in to small pieces. Brown the garlic in hot oil, add the meat and let it brown lightly on all sides. Add the tomatoes, wine, rosemary, pepper and salt. Simmer gently for 1½ hours or until the meat is tender.

SICILIAN STEWED VEAL VITELLO ALLA SICILIANA

2–2½ lb. breast of veal
flour for coating
1 large red pimiento
1 chopped clove of garlic
1 saltspoon cayenne, or a few drops of tabasco
2 oz. stoned black olives
salt
1 gill Chianti or other red wine
½ pint veal stock
oil for frying

Coat the veal with flour. Heat the oil, add the garlic and veal and cook until lightly browned. Remove the seeds and membranes from the pimiento; chop it coarsely and cook it in the oil for 5 minutes. Add the olives, wine, veal stock and seasoning. Put the lid on the saucepan and simmer very gently until the meat is tender (from 1–1½ hours).

Meat

HOLLOW BONE STEW OSSO BUCCO

3–4 lb. shin of veal	1 tablespoon tomato concentrate
seasoned flour	1 bay leaf
2 large chopped onions	1–1½ pints hot veal stock
2 chopped carrots	juice of 1 lemon
2 chopped celery stalks	butter for frying
2 chopped cloves of garlic	chopped parsley
pepper and salt	

The meat should be sawn into pieces about 2–2½ inches long. Coat them with seasoned flour. Cook in hot butter until they are brown all over. Add the vegetables; let them soften. Add the stock and bay leaf, stir in the tomato concentrate, season to taste. Simmer gently for 50–60 minutes, until the meat is tender. Add the lemon juice. Serve sprinkled with chopped parsley and serve with a plain risotto (see page 69). The marrow from the bones should be eaten.

SALTIMBOCCA

Saltimbocca literally means 'jump in the mouth'; in other words, it is so good it requires no effort to eat.

4 thin slices of veal cut from the leg	1 crushed clove of garlic
	pepper and salt
4 slices of prosciutto (raw ham), or thin slices of raw gammon	butter for frying
	1 gill of Marsala or sherry
4 sage leaves	

Get the butcher to flatten the meat. Rub it with garlic, season with pepper and salt. Put a sage leaf on each slice of veal and top with a slice of raw ham; keep it in place with a toothpick. Cook in hot butter until the meat is golden brown. Add the Marsala or sherry, then let it cook slowly for 15–20 minutes. Serve with the gravy from the pan.

Meat

BOCCONCINI

This is another version of saltimbocca. A slice of Gruyère is put between the veal and ham. After frying it, it is cooked in tomato sauce.

4 thin slices of veal
4 slices of raw ham
4 small slices of Gruyère
butter for frying
1 gill of freshly-made tomato sauce (see pages 151, 152)
pepper and salt

Fasten the meat, cheese and ham together with a toothpick. Fry in butter, add the tomato sauce and simmer for 15–20 minutes. Adjust the seasoning.

FARSUMAGRU

½ lb. chipolata sausages
1½–2 lb. breast of veal
2 large chopped onions
2 chopped cloves of garlic
2 hard-boiled eggs
2 tablespoons parsley
2 tablespoons tomato concentrate
½ pint veal stock made from bones
pepper and salt
¼ lb. Mozzarella or Bel Paese cheese
oil for frying

Bone the veal and cut it into small pieces. Soften the onions in hot oil. Put the veal, onions, garlic and parsley in a fireproof dish. Season well with pepper and salt. Arrange the sausages and the hard-boiled eggs, cut in rounds, on top. Add the tomato concentrate to the hot stock, stir to mix, pour it over the veal and sausages. Cover and cook in a slow oven (300°F–350°F) for 1½ hours or until the meat is tender. Remove the lid, cover the meat with slices of cheese and brown under the griller.

GENOESE STUFFED VEAL CIMA ALLA GENOVESE

1–1½ lb. boned breast or leg of veal, flattened and sewn up to make a 'bag' for the stuffing.

Meat

For the Stuffing

1 small chopped onion	1 tablespoon chopped marjoram or oregano
1 chopped clove of garlic	
1 veal sweetbread soaked in cold water, then blanched and chopped coarsely	2 beaten eggs
	pepper and salt
	grated Parmesan cheese
2 oz. each of chopped pork and ham	butter
4 oz. cooked shelled green peas	

Mix all the stuffing ingredients well together. Spread the mixture on the veal, then sew up the opening; make sure that none of the stuffing can come out while it is cooking. Stew the joint gently in salted water for 1–1½ hours. It can be served hot or cold. If it is to be served cold, let it cool in the water, remove, wrap it in grease-proof paper or foil, put a weight on top and leave for 2–3 hours. Serve cut in slices. Remember to remove the thread.

STUFFED VEAL ROLLS MESSICANI

1 lb. veal escalopes cut thin and well flattened	1 finely-chopped clove of garlic
	1 beaten egg
4 chopped rashers of streaky bacon	4 fresh sage leaves
	pepper, salt and nutmeg
½ lb. minced lean pork	2 tablespoons Marsala
1 oz. grated Parmesan cheese	1 gill stock
1 tablespoon chopped parsley	olive oil for frying

Mix together the bacon, pork, cheese, parsley and garlic. Season to taste with pepper, salt and nutmeg. Bind with the egg. Cut the escalopes into strips, 4 inches by 2 inches. Put some of the farce on each one, lay half a leaf of sage on top, roll up and tie with thread. Put the rolls on skewers (2–3 rolls on each); these should be short ones so that they fit into the frying-pan. Fry the rolls in hot olive oil all over so that they are nicely brown. Add the wine and stock, cover and cook gently for 30 minutes. If necessary, add a little more wine or stock. Correct the seasoning and serve hot.

Poultry and Game

IL POLLAME E LA CACCIAGIONE

Chicken Breasts Lombardy Style	*Petti di Pollo Alla Lombarda*
Chicken Breasts from Valdostana	*Pettio di Pollo Alla Valdostana*
Chicken Diavola	*Pollo Alla Diavola*
Chicken Hunter Style	*Pollo Alla Cacciatora*
Chicken with Olives	*Pollo Con Olive*
Chicken Stuffed with Pine Nuts	*Pollo Ripiene con Pignoli*
Chicken and Rice Salad	*Insalata di Pollo e Riso*
Chicken with Tuna Fish Sauce	*Pollo Tonnato*
Chicken with Pimientos	*Pollo con Peperoni*
Duck with Macaroni	*Anitra con Pappardelle*
Roast Duck with Olives	*Anitra Arrosto con Olive*
Roast Guinea Fowl with Candied Fruit	*Faraona Arrosta con Frutta Candita*
Salmi of Hare	*Salmi di Lepre*
Roast Kid	*Capretto al Forno*
Rabbit with Sweet-Sour Sauce	*Coniglio Al'Agro-Dolce*
Rabbit Hunter Style	*Coniglio alla Cacciatora*
Young Partridges Milan Style	*Perniciotte alla Milanese*
Boiled Turkey	*Tacchino Bollito*
Roast Venison	*Cervo Arrosto*
Venison Chops with Cream Sauce	*Costolette di Selvaggina Val d'Adige*

Poultry and Game
IL POLLAME E LA CACCIAGIONE

As in most warm countries, many mediocre hens peck a living from the countryside, although now there are more and more battery hens. Many recipes are for the breasts only; the rest of the bird is used for stews and soups.

The Italians have no sentimental feeling towards small birds, and so they shoot and cook almost everything that flies. There are recipes for birds of all sizes, from the thrush to the turkey.

CHICKEN BREASTS LOMBARDY STYLE PETTI DI POLLO ALLA LOMBARDA

Allow half a chicken breast per person.

2 chicken breasts skinned and cut in half lengthwise	1 tablespoon olive oil
a little flour	1 lb. shelled young peas
1 finely-sliced onion	2–3 chicken livers
1 dessertspoon chopped parsley	2 egg yolks
1 teaspoon fennel seeds	juice of ½ lemon
1 oz. butter	2 tablespoons Marsala
	pepper and salt

Brown the onion, parsley and fennel seeds in the hot butter and oil. Lightly flour the chicken fillets and fry them until brown on both sides. Add the hot stock, cover and simmer for 15 minutes. Add the peas and chopped chicken livers, season to taste, then add the Marsala. Cook for a further 10 minutes. Beat the egg yolks and lemon juice lightly together. Remove the pan from

Poultry and Game

the heat and gradually stir in the blended egg yolks and lemon. Serve at once.

CHICKEN BREASTS FROM VALDOSTANA PETTI DI POLLO ALLA VALDOSTANA

2 chicken breasts skinned and cut in half lengthwise
4 oz. white truffles, fresh or tinned, or, failing this, black truffles or mushrooms
2 oz. butter
6 oz. Mozarella or Bel Paese or Gruyère cheese
1 gill dry white wine
1 gill veal or chicken stock
pepper and salt
beaten egg and breadcrumbs for coating

Beat the chicken breasts flat. Finely slice the truffles or mushrooms, slice the cheese finely. Lay the truffles and cheese on the breasts and season to taste, then roll them up and tie with thread or secure with wooden toothpicks. Coat with beaten egg and breadcrumbs. Fry on all sides in the butter until brown. Add the wine and stock, cover the pan and cook gently for 30 minutes. Serve with the sauce poured round.

CHICKEN DIAVOLA POLLO ALLA DIAVOLA

2 young frying-chickens
pepper and salt
butter for frying
lemon juice

Split the cleaned chickens in half, flatten them well, season with pepper and salt. Melt plenty of butter in a large heavy frying-pan; cook the chicken halves for 6 minutes each side fairly quickly. Reduce the heat and continue to cook for 15–20 minutes, basting and turning frequently. They should be cooked in this time if they are really young. Serve sprinkled with lemon juice. This is a simple but very delicious way of cooking chickens. Ideally they should be cooked *on* a hot grill.

Poultry and Game

CHICKEN HUNTER STYLE POLLO ALLA CACCIATORA

1 chicken (3½–4 lb.)
1 large chopped onion
2 chopped cloves of garlic
1 chopped pimiento, seeds and
    membrane removed
1 lb. skinned, chopped tomatoes
2 tablespoons tomato concentrate
1 bay leaf
pepper and salt
1 gill red wine
chicken stock made from giblets
oil for frying

Joint the chicken. Brown the pieces in hot oil, add the onion, garlic and pimiento and cook for 5–6 minutes. Add the tomatoes, bay leaf, red wine, pepper and salt. Add enough chicken stock just to cover the chicken; when it is hot, stir in the tomato concentrate. Simmer gently for 40–45 minutes or until the chicken is tender.

CHICKEN WITH OLIVES POLLO CON OLIVE

1 chicken (3½–4 lb.)
1 chopped onion
1 chopped carrot
12 large, stoned, black olives
3 tablespoons tomato concentrate
3 skinned, chopped tomatoes
pepper and salt (if olives are not
    too salt)
1 bay leaf
chicken stock made from giblets
oil for frying

Brown the chicken on all sides in hot oil. Add the onion and carrot; cook for 5 minutes. Add the tomatoes, olives, bay leaf and enough chicken stock to cover the chicken; when it is hot, add the tomato concentrate. Simmer gently for 40–45 minutes or until the chicken is tender. Correct the seasoning.

CHICKEN STUFFED WITH PINE NUTS POLLO RIPIENE CON PIGNOLI

Pine nuts are available from many health food stores and some Italian shops.

1 roasting-chicken (4 lb.)
pepper and salt
melted butter

Poultry and Game

For the Stuffing

1 small chopped onion
1 chopped clove of garlic
1 dessertspoon chopped parsley
4 chopped rashers of streaky bacon
2 chopped hard-boiled eggs

1 slightly-beaten egg
4 oz. pine nuts
2 tablespoons cooked rice
pepper and salt

Mix all the ingredients together and bind with the beaten egg. Add pepper and salt to taste. Stuff the chicken, season with pepper and salt, coat with melted butter and put it in a casserole. Cover and cook in a moderate oven (350°F–375°F) for 1½ hours or until tender. Because the chicken is stuffed, it takes longer to cook.

CHICKEN AND RICE SALAD INSALATA DI POLLO E RISO

cold cooked chicken cut in cubes
chopped, tender, crisp celery stalks
2 large cups cooked rice
strips of red and green pimientos

oil
lemon juice
freshly-ground black pepper
salt

Mix the chicken, celery, rice and pimientos together. Season liberally with olive oil, a little lemon juice, pepper and salt.

CHICKEN WITH TUNA FISH SAUCE POLLO TONNATO

This is made in the same way as Vitello Tonnato (see page 116); but instead of veal, slices of cold cooked chicken are covered with a fish sauce.

CHICKEN WITH PIMIENTOS POLLO CON PEPERONI

1 jointed chicken (4 lb.)
2 chopped onions
1 chopped clove of garlic
3 sliced pimientos
3 tablespoons tomato concentrate

a pinch of dried rosemary
pepper and salt
1 gill white wine
water
oil for frying

Brown the onion and garlic in hot oil. Add chicken joints and brown them all over. Add the pimientos, rosemary, pepper, salt and white wine, then add enough water to cover the chicken; when it is hot stir in the tomato concentrate. Simmer gently until the chicken is tender (45–50 minutes).

DUCK WITH MACARONI ANITRA CON PAPPARDELLE

Pappardelle is like tagliatelle, only wider; but if you cannot get it, use ordinary macaroni.

1 young jointed duck
1 lb. peeled and quartered tomatoes
1 gill red wine
1 bay leaf
3–4 juniper berries
oil
1 dessertspoon chopped fresh marjoram, or a good pinch of dried marjoram
pepper and salt
¾ lb. boiled macaroni

Cook the tomatoes in hot oil, squashing them with a wooden spoon until they are soft. Add the duck, wine, herbs and seasoning. Chop the duck liver very finely and add it to the sauce. Simmer for 1–1½ hours or until the duck is tender. Serve with the sauce and the macaroni.

ROAST DUCK WITH OLIVES ANITRA ARROSTO CON OLIVE

1 small duck (about 4 lb.)   *pepper and salt*

Season the duck with pepper and salt. Prick the skin all over with a skewer; this allows the fat to run off. Roast in a hot oven (425°F–450°F) for about 1 hour or until the duck is cooked to your liking. While the duck is cooking, make the sauce.

For the Sauce

2 finely-chopped onions
chopped liver and heart of the duck
butter for frying
¾ pint beef or chicken stock
pepper and salt
2–3 oz. stoned black olives

Fry the onions in butter until they are soft and beginning to brown. Add the liver and heart and fry for 10 minutes. Add the stock, pepper and salt to taste and the olives. Simmer gently until the duck is cooked. Serve the duck with flat noodles, and the sauce separately.

ROAST GUINEA FOWL WITH CANDIED FRUIT
FARAONA ARROSTA CON FRUTTA CANDITA

I first ate guinea fowl with candied fruit on an Italian ship. It may sound odd, but this rather dry bird was greatly improved by this accompaniment. Fruit with poultry crops up in the wonderful German dish of roast chicken served with a compôte of tinned fruit—peaches, cherries, pineapple and plums. In both cases the combination of fruit and fowl is fascinating.

1 guinea fowl
candied fruits (such as cherries, apricots, pineapple, melon and angelica), or

Mostarda di Frutta (mustard-flavoured candied fruit in syrup) (see page 155)
fat bacon

Cover the breast of the bird with plenty of fat bacon. Roast it in a hot oven (450°F) for 35–40 minutes. Remove the bacon 20 minutes before the bird is cooked, so that the breast is browned. Serve it with buttered new potatoes and follow with a green salad. Tiny individual bowls of the chopped candied fruit are put beside each person.

SALMI OF HARE SALMI DI LEPRE

1 small young hare, cleaned, skinned and jointed
a little flour
olive oil
1 sliced lemon
1 chopped clove of garlic
1 chopped carrot

2 chopped celery stalks
a sprig of rosemary
2 cloves
pepper and salt
½ pint red wine or a mixture of wine and stock

Make a marinade with the vegetables, rosemary, cloves, pepper, salt and wine, add the pieces of hare and leave them overnight. The next day remove the hare, drain well, dust lightly with flour and fry in hot oil until brown all over. Add the vegetables and the marinade. Simmer gently for 1–1½ hours, until the hare is tender. Correct the seasoning. Serve hot with noodles or boiled or fried polenta. If liked, the liver and heart can be added to the marinade.

ROAST KID CAPRETTO AL FORNO

Occasionally one has the chance to buy kid. The flesh is tender and has an unusual flavour; it is well worth trying.

a small roasting-joint of kid, (leg, forequarter or haunch)

larding bacon

For the Marinade

1 chopped onion
1 chopped clove of garlic
2 sliced carrots
2 chopped sticks of celery
1 gill red wine
1 tablespoon wine vinegar
a sprinkling of thyme

a good pinch each of nutmeg and ginger
a few coriander seeds
1 tablespoon chopped tarragon
pepper and salt
water

Put the joint in a large earthenware dish or bowl; cover with the marinade; add enough water to cover the meat. Leave for 24 hours, turning occasionally. Remove the joint from the marinade, dry well and cover with fat bacon. Cook in a hot oven (420°F–440°F); allow 20 minutes per lb. While the meat is cooking, make the sauce: cook the marinade until it has reduced by half, then strain it and serve separately.

RABBIT WITH SWEET-SOUR SAUCE CONIGLIO AL' AGRO DOLCE

1 jointed rabbit

For the Sweet-Sour Sauce

3 tablespoons wine vinegar
3 tablespoons sugar
2 tablespoons tomato concentrate
6 stoned, finely-chopped green olives

2 finely-chopped celery stalks
1 tablespoon capers
pepper and salt
1 cup water

Poultry and Game

Mix all the ingredients together. Pour the sauce over the rabbit. Cook gently until the rabbit is tender (about 1–1¼ hours).

RABBIT HUNTER STYLE CONIGLIO ALLA CACCIATORA

1 jointed rabbit
1 large chopped onion
1 chopped carrot
1 chopped clove of garlic
1 lb. skinned, chopped tomatoes
½ teaspoon dried rosemary
1 gill red wine
1 tablespoon tomato concentrate
stock
pepper and salt
oil for frying

Brown the rabbit in the hot oil. Add the onion, garlic and carrot and brown them. Now add the wine, tomatoes, rosemary, pepper and salt to taste, and enough stock to cover the rabbit; when it is hot add the tomato concentrate. Simmer gently until the rabbit is tender (about 1–1½ hours).

YOUNG PARTRIDGES MILAN STYLE PERNICIOTTE ALLA MILANESE

2 young partridges split in half
olive oil
sprig of rosemary
1 bay leaf
3–4 juniper berries
pepper and salt
flour
beaten egg
fine brown breadcrumbs

Flatten the half partridges. Add the rosemary, bay leaf, juniper berries, pepper and salt to the oil and marinate the birds for 2–3 hours, turning them over occasionally so that they become impregnated. Drain them, dip the halves in flour, egg and breadcrumbs and fry in hot olive oil for about 20 minutes; the time will depend on how young the birds are. Serve with anchovy sauce (see next page).

Poultry and Game

For the Anchovy Sauce

1 small tin anchovy fillets	2 tablespoons finely-chopped parsley
2 tablespoons olive oil, plus the oil from the tinned anchovies	mashed yolks of 3 hard-boiled eggs
2 tablespoons wine vinegar	freshly-ground black pepper
1 chopped clove of garlic	

Pound the garlic and anchovies into a paste; add the parsley. Heat the oil a little; add the paste, stirring and cooking slowly. Add alternately the vinegar and egg yolks; blend until smooth. Remove from the heat. This sauce can be served hot with hot dishes or cold with cold meat or fish.

BOILED TURKEY TACCHINO BOLLITO

The Italians make many interesting dishes with the breasts of turkey. They often stuff a turkey and roast it as we do. More unusual is boiled turkey. I have eaten this in the North of Italy and liked it very much.

1 really small turkey	2 chopped cloves of garlic
4 chopped onions	2–3 chopped celery stalks
2 chopped carrots	2 quarts of stock made from the turkey giblets and trimmings
1 lb. skinned and quartered tomatoes	pepper and salt

For the Sauce

1 quart of turkey stock	½ lb. minced mushrooms
2 oz. butter	1 gill white wine
2 oz. flour	pepper and salt

If you have not a large enough pan to hold the turkey, you could joint it. Put the turkey in a saucepan, add the stock, bring to the boil, remove scum, then add the vegetables, pepper and salt. Simmer gently for 2–2½ hours or until the turkey is tender. Melt the butter, add the flour and cook for 3–4 minutes without browning; add the strained turkey stock, stir and cook for a few minutes, then add the minced mushrooms and the wine. Cook gently for 15 minutes. Check the seasoning.

ROAST VENISON CERVO ARROSTO

Choose a cut from the haunch, the loin or the best end of neck. Marinate it (see below) for 24 hours before cooking. Then rub salt and pepper, and a little ginger if liked, over the joint. Wrap in aluminium foil and cook it in a moderate oven (350°F–375°F); allow 20–30 minutes per pound. Remove the foil 20 minutes before it is done. Baste well and let it brown. Carve it like lamb.

1½ *lb. venison (haunch, loin or best end of neck)*

For the Marinade

1 *chopped onion*	1 *tablespoon olive oil*
1 *chopped clove of garlic*	8 *crushed juniper berries*
1 *bay leaf*	1 *small glass of Marsala*
a sprig of thyme and of parsley	*pepper and salt*
1 *tablespoon wine vinegar*	*enough water to cover the meat*

Put all the ingredients in a deep dish, then put in the meat; turn it frequently so that it is well soaked. Drain well before roasting. Bring the marinade to the boil, reduce it by half, strain and serve with the roast.

VENISON CHOPS WITH CREAM SAUCE COSTOLETTE DI SELVAGGINA VAL D'ADIGE

4 *venison chops cut* 1 *inch thick*	*chestnut purée*
pepper and salt	*cream sauce*

Season the chops with pepper and salt. Grill them for 20–25 minutes, turning frequently. Serve with chestnut purée (see page 141) and cream sauce.

Poultry and Game

For the Cream Sauce (Salsa Bianca)

1 small chopped onion	1 gill milk
1 oz. butter	5 fluid oz. cream
½ oz. flour	pepper and salt
2 oz. finely-sliced mushrooms	

Fry the onion in hot butter until it softens. Add the mushrooms; cook until they are soft. Sprinkle in the flour; stir and cook for 2–3 minutes; do not let the flour brown. Slowly add the milk, stirring all the time. Cook until the sauce is smooth and creamy, then stir in the cream and let it heat slowly. Correct the seasoning. Serve the chops with the sauce poured over.

Vegetables

VERDURA

Artichokes Jewish Style	*Carciofi alla Giudia*
Baked Globe Artichokes	*Carciofi al Forno*
Asparagus	*Asparagi*
Asparagus with Parmesan	*Asparagi alla Parmigiana*
Baked Aubergine or Egg Plant	*Melanzane al Forno*
Fried Aubergines	*Melanzane Fritte*
Broccoli	*Broccoli*
French Beans	*Fagiolini*
Sharp Cabbage	*Cavolo Agro*
Cauliflower Soufflé	*Soufflé di Cavolfiore*
Fried Courgettes	*Zucchini Fritti*
Stewed Courgettes	*Zucchini in Stufato*
Stuffed Courgettes	*Zucchini Ripiene*
Chestnut Purée	*Purea di Castagne*
Stewed Chestnuts	*Castagne in Stufato*
Chick Peas	*Ceci*
Stuffed Onions	*Cipolle Ripiene*
Carrots with Marsala	*Carote al Marsala*
Stuffed Mushrooms	*Funghi Ripieni*
Mushrooms Trifolati	*Funghi Trifolati*
Peas with Ham	*Piselli con Prosciutto*
Pimientos and Tomatoes	*Peperonata*
Potato Croquettes	*Crocchette di Patate*
Potatoes with Milk	*Patate al Latte*
Fried Potatoes with Rosemary	*Patate Fritte con Rosmarino*
Spinach Croquettes	*Crocchette di Spinaci*
Spinach Pudding	*Sformato di Spinaci*

Vegetables

Spinach with Parmesan Cheese	*Spinaci alla Parmigiana*
Spinach Roman Style	*Spinaci alla Romana*
Florentine Pasties	*Torta alla Fiorentina*
Turnips Stewed in Stock	*Broada*

Vegetables
VERDURA

In Italy vegetables are always fresh, young and imaginatively cooked. Plates piled high with badly-cooked potatoes and one or two other overcooked vegetables are virtually unknown. Vegetables and salads are served as dishes in their own right, sometimes before, and sometimes after, the main course. Very often spinach, beet tops, broccoli and similar vegetables are served cold or lukewarm, dressed with olive oil and a little lemon juice, and very good they are. Delectable vegetable moulds (sformati) make a light and nourishing meal.

They have grass-like wild asparagus and large thick white ones. Globe artichokes (carciofi), purplish and green, large and small, are always tender. Then there are delicious baby marrows (zucchini) and the sweetest of tiny green peas (piselli), also broad beans (fave) so crisp and juicy that they are eaten raw.

There are plenty of aubergines and pimientos of various hues, shapes and sizes. These are easily obtainable in England, and although they may seem expensive, there is very little waste with them. The addition of one or two gives variety to everyday dishes. Also these vegetables are rich in vitamins.

I always buy cauliflowers called Pisa Points when I can. They are a creamy-yellow colour, very attractive, with pointed whorls. Their flavour is much more delicate than that of English cauliflowers. My local greengrocer says he has a job to sell them as most of his customers, not being accustomed to the look of them, are chary of buying them.

The prosaic cabbage becomes an elegant dish when it is lightly cooked and served in a sweet and sour sauce, or if the leaves are stuffed.

Vegetables

I have never been able to understand why we concentrate on growing enormous vegetables, sacrificing flavour for size, when the Italians and the French aim for small succulent ones. I suppose mass psychologists would read something into this national characteristic.

The ubiquitous tomato, a native of Peru, was first grown in Italy and from there spread over Europe in the latter half of the sixteenth century. It is used in so many Italian dishes, but to my mind never becomes monotonous.

ARTICHOKES JEWISH STYLE CARCIOFI ALLA GIUDIA

This speciality of the Roman Jews has become a classic. The success of the dish really depends on the tenderness of the artichokes; it is difficult to buy them young enough in England. They are fried in oil and flattened out so that they look like crisp flowers. The whole artichoke is eaten.

4 *globe artichokes*	*lemon juice*
olive oil for deep-frying	*pepper and salt*

Leave the stalks on the artichokes, but trim them. Remove the large outside leaves and snip off the tops of the other leaves with a sharp pair of scissors. Open out the artichoke as far as possible; if they are not very young, remove the choke. Wash them in water and lemon juice. Drain well. Have a deep pan full of very hot oil and put in the artichokes, head down. Fry over a medium heat for 9–10 minutes, turning them over occasionally. Remove and drain well. Leave them for 30 minutes—longer if convenient. Reheat the oil; hold each artichoke by the stalk and put it in gently. The leaves will curl back and the artichoke be a beautiful rich brown and really crisp. Remove from the oil, season quickly with pepper and salt. Serve with the stalks uppermost.

Vegetables

BAKED GLOBE ARTICHOKES CARCIOFI AL FORNO

4 globe artichokes	pepper and salt
2 chopped cloves of garlic	olive oil
2 tablespoons chopped parsley	½ pint hot water
2 tablespoons butter	melted butter

Wash the artichokes, cut off the stems and the tips of the leaves. Pound the garlic, parsley, butter, pepper and salt together until smooth, put little dabs of this mixture in between the leaves, then put the artichokes in a fireproof dish, pour in the hot water and sprinkle the artichokes with olive oil. Cover the dish and cook in a moderate oven (350°F) until they are tender. The time required will be between 30 and 50 minutes, depending upon the age of the artichokes. To test, insert a fork or skewer into the base. Serve with melted butter.

ASPARAGUS ASPARAGI

The wild asparagus found near Rome is tender and sweet and at its best plain boiled with melted butter. To my mind it is spoiled when served with Parmesan cheese.

ASPARAGUS WITH PARMESAN ASPARAGI ALLA PARMIGIANA

1–1½ lb. lightly-boiled asparagus	butter
grated Parmesan cheese	

Lay the cooked asparagus in a shallow fireproof dish. Cover plentifully with Parmesan cheese. Put small pieces of butter on top and grill quickly until the top is brown.

Vegetables

BAKED AUBERGINES OR EGGPLANTS MELANZANE AL FORNO

2 large or 4 small aubergines
olive oil
1 finely-chopped onion
1 finely-chopped clove of garlic
2 large slices of bread, without crusts, soaked in milk
1 egg yolk
pepper
2 chopped anchovy fillets
6 stoned, chopped black olives
1 tablespoon chopped parsley or marjoram

Remove the stalks and parboil the aubergines for 15 minutes in salted water, then cut them in halves lengthwise and scoop out the flesh without breaking the skin. Fry the onion and garlic in the hot oil until lightly browned. Squeeze the moisture from the bread; mash the aubergine flesh and mix the aubergine, bread, pepper, garlic, anchovies, olives and parsley or marjoram together. Add this mixture to the onion and garlic; cook and stir for 5 minutes. Remove from the heat, then stir in the beaten egg yolk. Put the aubergine shells in a fireproof dish, fill them with the stuffing, sprinkle with olive oil. Cook in a moderate oven (350°F–375°F) for about 40–45 minutes.

FRIED AUBERGINES MELANZANE FRITTE

1 medium-sized aubergine
flour
lightly-beaten egg
oil for frying

Peel and cut the aubergine into ½-inch slices. Dredge them with flour, dip in beaten egg and fry slowly in hot oil until they are golden-brown (about 5–6 minutes each side).

BROCCOLI BROCCOLI

3–4 broccoli (or 1 small cauliflower)
olive oil
2 finely-chopped cloves of garlic
pepper and salt
chopped parsley

Trim the broccoli (or cauliflower), break into small flowerets, cut the stems into small pieces. Cook gently in boiling salted water for

5–6 minutes; it must be slightly undercooked. Drain well. Heat a little olive oil in a frying-pan; add the garlic and let it brown, then add the broccoli and cook for 5 minutes. Add pepper and salt to taste and chopped parsley.

FRENCH BEANS FAGIOLINI

1 lb. young French beans
1 tablespoon butter
1 tablespoon olive oil
1 small sliced onion
1 chopped clove of garlic
pepper and salt

Prepare the beans by breaking off the stalks and tips; remove any strings. Cook in boiling salted water until tender, but do not overcook them. Drain well. Soften the onion and garlic in the butter and oil; add the beans, pepper and salt and stir over a low heat for 1 or 2 minutes. Serve hot.

SHARP CABBAGE CAVOLO AGRO

1 young cabbage
3 chopped rashers of bacon
1 pint water
1 tablespoon white wine vinegar
pepper and salt
1 teaspoon fennel seeds

Wash and shred the cabbage. Fry the bacon until the fat runs; add the cabbage, water, vinegar, pepper, salt and fennel seeds. Cook fairly slowly, stirring occasionally, until the cabbage is tender. Most of the liquid will have evaporated and the cabbage will have a refreshing piquant flavour.

CAULIFLOWER SOUFFLÉ SOUFFLÉ DI CAVOLFIORE

1 cauliflower
1½ tablespoons butter
1½ tablespoons flour
½ pint milk
4 lightly-beaten egg yolks
4 stiffly-beaten egg whites
pepper and salt
grated nutmeg
2 tablespoons grated Parmesan cheese

Wash the cauliflower and break it into flowerets. Cook it in boiling salted water, drain well, then put it through a vegetable mill or

Vegetables

rub through a sieve. Melt the butter; add the flour, stirring until the fat is absorbed; add the hot milk; season to taste with pepper, salt and nutmeg; add the cauliflower, egg yolks and cheese; fold in the egg whites. Put the mixture in a buttered soufflé dish or a deep round tin. Cook in a moderately hot oven (350°F) for about 20 minutes or until the soufflé is well risen. Serve at once.

FRIED COURGETTES ZUCCHINI FRITTI

$1\frac{1}{2}$ lb. courgettes
oil for frying
wine vinegar

pepper and salt
chopped mint

Do not peel the courgettes. Cut them in rounds and fry in oil until tender (about 4 minutes). Drain well. Season with pepper, salt, a little wine vinegar and finely-chopped mint.

STEWED COURGETTES ZUCCHINI IN STUFATO

1 lb. unpeeled courgettes cut in rounds
4 finely-sliced onions
2 finely-chopped cloves of garlic

$\frac{1}{2}$ lb. peeled, chopped tomatoes, or a small tin
pepper and salt
olive oil

Fry the onions and garlic in hot oil until lightly browned. Add the tomatoes and courgettes. Season to taste. Simmer until the courgettes are cooked (25–30 minutes).

STUFFED COURGETTES ZUCCHINI RIPIENI

8–10 courgettes
1 large slice of bread (crust removed), soaked in milk and squeezed dry
3–4 chopped mushrooms
2 chopped anchovy fillets
2 diced slices of raw ham

1 tablespoon grated Parmesan cheese
1 teaspoon chopped fresh basil, marjoram or parsley
1 egg yolk
oil

Vegetables

Cook the courgettes in boiling salted water for 3 minutes. Drain well and cut them in halves lengthwise. Scoop out the pulp with a teaspoon and mix it with the bread, mushrooms, anchovies, ham, cheese, herbs, egg yolk and pepper. Fill the courgette halves. Put them in a greased fireproof dish, sprinkle with oil and bake in a moderate oven (375°F) for 35–40 minutes.

CHESTNUT PURÉE PUREA DI CASTAGNE

Italian chestnuts are amongst the best in the world. The Italians make full use of them, for both savoury and sweet dishes, as they realize how nourishing they are.

1 lb. chestnuts *milk*
pepper and salt *butter*

Make a nick in each chestnut near the point. Put them in a moderately slow oven for 15–20 minutes. As soon as they are cool enough to handle, remove the shells. Cook them in boiling salted water until they are tender (about 30 minutes). Drain, and remove the second skin. Mash the chestnuts thoroughly until they are smooth, add enough hot milk to make a purée, then add a good piece of butter and pepper and salt to taste. Heat over a low flame, beating to mix in the butter and seasoning. Serve hot.

STEWED CHESTNUTS CASTAGNE IN STUFATO

1 lb. prepared chestnuts (see *3 chopped sticks of celery*
previous recipe) *water*
pepper and salt

Cook the peeled chestnuts, with the celery, in boiling salted water until they are tender (about 30 minutes). When they are done, drain well, season with pepper and serve with melted butter.

CHICK PEAS CECI

Chick peas need a long soaking and a lot of cooking. To save this trouble they can be bought in tins, already cooked. They

Vegetables

can be prepared and served in various ways: in salads, with sauces and with rice as in Risi e Bisi (see page 41).

½ lb. chick peas soaked overnight	3 chopped anchovy fillets
1 chopped onion	pepper
2 chopped cloves of garlic	pinch of cinnamon
oil	pinch of saffron
1 bay leaf	chopped parsley
1 lb. peeled and quartered tomatoes	

Cook the chick peas in boiling salted water until they are tender. While they are cooking, soften the onion in hot oil, then add the garlic, tomatoes, bay leaf, anchovy fillets, pepper, cinnamon and saffron. Simmer until you have a thick purée, then add the drained chick peas and simmer for 10 minutes. Serve sprinkled with chopped parsley.

STUFFED ONIONS CIPOLLE RIPIENE

4 large onions	1 beaten egg
½ lb. finely-minced veal or beef	pepper and salt
1 thick slice of bread soaked in milk	½ pint tomato sauce (see pages 151, 152)
¼ lb. finely-chopped mushrooms	

Peel the onions. Boil them gently in salted water, for about 20–25 minutes, until they begin to soften. Remove and drain them; let them cool. Remove the centre of each onion; this can be done with a blunt knife. Chop the onion centres and mix them with the meat, mushrooms, pepper and salt. Squeeze the moisture from the bread, then add the bread and the beaten egg. Put some of the stuffing into each onion case. Bake in a greased fireproof dish for 20–25 minutes in a moderately hot oven (350°F–375°F). Serve with tomato sauce poured over.

CARROTS WITH MARSALA CAROTE AL MARSALA

1–1½ lb. young carrots	butter
3–4 tablespoons Marsala (or sherry)	pepper and salt
	chopped parsley

Vegetables

Divide the washed carrots lengthwise into four. Cook them in boiling salted water until they are just cooked. Drain them. Melt some butter in a heavy saucepan, toss the carrots in it, season with pepper and salt, add the Marsala and cook for 2–3 minutes. Serve sprinkled with chopped parsley.

STUFFED MUSHROOMS FUNGHI RIPIENI

12 large mushrooms
1 finely-chopped onion
3 finely-chopped cloves of garlic
2 tablespoons chopped parsley
3 chopped anchovy fillets
3 tablespoons fine brown breadcrumbs
pepper and salt
olive oil

Wipe the mushrooms. Remove the stalks and chop them finely; mix them with the anchovies, onion, garlic, parsley, breadcrumbs, pepper and salt. Arrange the mushrooms in a large fireproof dish, put some of the stuffing on each, sprinkle well with olive oil and pour a little oil in the dish. Cover and bake in a moderate oven (375°F) for 30 minutes. Baste occasionally while they are cooking.

MUSHROOMS TRIFOLATI FUNGHI TRIFOLATI

1 lb. mushrooms, thinly sliced
2 cloves of garlic
4 chopped anchovy fillets
freshly-ground black pepper
1 tablespoon chopped parsley
2 tablespoons olive oil
1 tablespoon butter
lemon juice

Fry the garlic in the hot oil until brown. Add the mushrooms and cook for 5–6 minutes. Pound the anchovies and butter together, add to the mushrooms and cook and stir for 2 minutes. Add pepper to taste and the parsley. Serve sprinkled with lemon juice.

PEAS WITH HAM PISELLI CON PROSCIUTTO

1½ lb. shelled fresh young green peas
4 slices prosciutto (raw ham) or raw lean gammon rashers
1 very finely-chopped onion
1 tablespoon butter
1 teaspoon sugar
pepper and salt

Vegetables

Cook the peas in a little boiling salted water. Drain them and keep the water. Melt the butter, cook the onion until it softens, add the ham or gammon and cook for a few minutes. Add the peas, sugar, pepper and about 1 gill of the vegetable water. Simmer for 4–5 minutes. Correct the seasoning; add a little salt if necessary.

PIMIENTOS AND TOMATOES PEPERONATA

6 red or yellow pimientos
2 lb. peeled and quartered tomatoes
2 medium-sized sliced onions
2 chopped cloves of garlic
pepper and salt
olive oil

Wipe the pimientos; remove the stalks, membranes and seeds; chop the pimientos coarsely. Cook the onions in hot oil until they soften and turn golden. Add the pimientos and garlic; cook for a few minutes, then add the tomatoes, pepper and salt. Simmer slowly for 1–1½ hours; the longer it cooks, the better it is. Serve hot or cold.

POTATO CROQUETTES CROCCHETTE DI PATATE

1½ lb. potatoes
1 beaten egg
2 oz. grated Parmesan cheese
1 tablespoon chopped parsley
pepper and salt
brown breadcrumbs
olive oil for frying

Scrub the potatoes; do not peel them. Boil them in salted water, then peel and mash them thoroughly while still hot. Add the egg, cheese, pepper, salt and parsley. Leave to cool, then form into balls or rissoles. Roll in breadcrumbs. Fry in hot oil until brown all over.

POTATOES WITH MILK PATATE AL LATTE

1½ lb. potatoes
½ pint milk
pepper and salt
nutmeg

Vegetables

Peel and boil the potatoes. Cut them into thin rounds. Put them in a buttered fireproof dish. Add pepper, salt and nutmeg to the milk and pour it over the potatoes. Bake them in a hot oven for 50–55 minutes or until they are cooked.

FRIED POTATOES WITH ROSEMARY PATATE FRITTE CON ROSMARINO

2 lb. potatoes
½ teaspoon dried rosemary

olive oil for deep-frying
salt

Peel the potatoes. Cut them into small cubes or strips. Fry them in hot oil with the rosemary until they are golden and cooked. Drain well, sprinkle with salt and serve at once.

SPINACH CROQUETTES CROCCHETTE DI SPINACI

1–1½ lb. cooked, well-drained spinach purée
1 beaten egg
2 oz. grated Parmesan cheese

a good pinch of nutmeg
pepper and salt
fine brown breadcrumbs
butter for frying

Mix together the spinach, egg, cheese, nutmeg, pepper and salt. Form into small balls; roll in breadcrumbs. Fry in hot butter until brown all over.

SPINACH PUDDING SFORMATO DI SPINACI

These vegetable 'puddings' are very like the French vegetable 'pain'. They can be made with different sorts of vegetables: lettuce, spinach, green peas and French beans. They make excellent entrées or supper dishes.

2 lb. cooked spinach purée
3 eggs
2 oz. butter
2 oz. flour

½ pint milk
1 oz. grated Parmesan cheese
pepper and salt
nutmeg

Make a thick sauce with the butter, flour and hot milk. Season

Vegetables

well and add the cheese and spinach. Let it cool, then add the beaten eggs. Pour into a buttered soufflé dish, deep round tin, or basin, and steam for about 1 hour. Serve hot.

SPINACH WITH PARMESAN CHEESE SPINACI ALLA PARMIGIANA

2 lb. cooked spinach	3 tablespoons grated Parmesan cheese
oil	
3 finely-chopped cloves of garlic	grated nutmeg, pepper and salt
3 lightly-beaten eggs	

Drain the spinach well and chop it finely. Melt the oil in a saucepan, brown the garlic, remove it, then add to the oil in the pan the spinach, nutmeg, pepper, salt, eggs and cheese. Mix well together. Cook and stir for 4–5 minutes. Serve hot.

SPINACH ROMAN STYLE SPINACI ALLA ROMANA

2 lb. spinach	olive oil
pepper and salt	lemon juice

Cook the washed spinach without water until it is tender. Drain very well, chop it and serve it cold with olive oil and lemon juice.

FLORENTINE PASTIES TORTA ALLA FIORENTINA

1 lb. cooked, well-drained spinach purée	2 oz. grated Parmesan cheese
3 oz. finely-chopped ham	1 egg

Mix all the ingredients well together.

For the Pastry

¾ lb. flour	1 egg yolk
pinch of salt	½ lb. butter

Mix together the flour (sifted with the salt) and the egg yolk and butter. Knead thoroughly. Leave in the refrigerator, or a cool place,

Vegetables

overnight or for a few hours. Roll out the pastry thinly, cut into rounds about 3 inches in diameter, put the stuffing on one half, fold the other half over, damp the edges and press well together. Cook in a hot oven (425°F) for 10 minutes, then reduce the heat to 350°F and cook for 10 minutes longer.

TURNIPS STEWED IN STOCK BROADA

1 *lb. peeled turnips*	1 *teaspoon sugar*
butter	1 *teaspoon flour*
pepper and salt	1 *gill hot meat stock*

Chop the turnips coarsely and cook them for 2–3 minutes in hot butter. Sprinkle over them the pepper, salt, sugar and flour; stir and cook for about 2 minutes. Add the hot stock and cook gently for 20 minutes or until the turnips are soft. Serve hot.

Sauces

SALSA

Almond Sauce	*Salsa di Mandorle*
Calabrian Sauce	*Salsa di Calabria*
Brown Sauce	*Salsa Bruna*
Green Sauce	*Salsa Verde*
Caper Sauce	*Salsa di Capperi*
Prawn Sauce	*Salsa di Gamberi*
Tomato Sauce (1)	*Salsa alla Pizzaiola*
Tomato Sauce (2)	*Salsa di Pomidoro*
Tomato and Meat Sauce	*Salsa di Pomidoro con Carne*
Hot Sauce	*La Bagna Cauda*
Sweet-Sour Sauce	*Salsa Agro-Dolce*
Sweet-Sour Sauce with Nuts	*Salsa Agro-Dolce con Noci*
Mayonnaise	*Maionese*
Tuna Fish Mayonnaise	*Maionese Tonnato*
Pesto	*Il Pesto*
Fruit Mustard	*Mostarda di Frutta*

Sauces

SALSA

The Italians, like the Indians and Chinese, have a gastronomic need to flavour their pleasant-tasting but relatively insipid staple foods. Italian sauces have developed from primitive beginnings and have never risen to the heights of French haute cuisine. This is no criticism—far from it, for in Italy they manage to make an infinite variety of virile sauces from the resources that are readily to hand. They have dozens of different tomato sauces and, except for colour, these really are different.

They make meat sauces to give extra nourishment to their pasta. They have sea-food, herb and sweet and sour sauces. The range is wide, from the delicate, subtle cream sauce served with Fettucine all'Alfredo to the boisterous blend of garlic, oregano, bacon and beaten egg which flavours Spaghetti alla Carbonara. Pounded tuna fish and anchovies are used to flavour cold veal and chicken.

In the south, strong-flavoured virgin olive oil gives a special tang; while in the north, butter produces suave and urbane undertones. I like Italian sauces, they suit the food, the climate and the people.

Apart from the sauces in this section, recipes for others are given with the dishes to which they are particularly well suited.

ALMOND SAUCE SALSA DI MANDORLE

2 oz. blanched, finely-chopped almonds
1 oz. butter
lemon juice
pepper and salt

Let the butter brown. Add the almonds, and lemon juice to taste. Season with pepper and salt. Serve with fish.

Sauces

CALABRIAN SAUCE SALSA DI CALABRIA

This is a variation of tomato sauce.

1 chopped onion
2 chopped cloves of garlic
1 small tin of anchovy fillets
1 small tin of tuna fish in olive oil
2½–3 lb. tomatoes
freshly-ground black pepper
salt if necessary
1 tablespoon finely-chopped fresh basil, marjoram or parsley
1 tablespoon olive oil

Heat the oil and cook the onion and garlic until they soften and change colour. Chop the anchovies coarsely and add them with the oil from the tin. Add the tomatoes, peeled and chopped, and let them cook slowly; when they have reduced and the sauce has thickened, add the flaked tuna fish, the pepper and a little salt if necessary. Stir and cook slowly for 10 minutes. Lastly, add the chopped basil, marjoram or parsley. Serve hot with pasta.

BROWN SAUCE SALSA BRUNA

1 chopped onion
1 chopped clove of garlic
1½ oz. butter
1½ oz. flour
pepper and salt
1 pint beef stock
1 bay leaf
1 teaspoon chopped marjoram
1 teaspoon chopped parsley

Heat the butter and cook the onion and garlic until they brown. Add the flour; let it brown, but take care not to let it burn. Gradually add the hot stock, stirring all the time, then add the bay leaf, marjoram and parsley, with pepper and salt to taste. Simmer for 20 minutes. Strain before using.

GREEN SAUCE SALSA VERDE

a good handful of chopped parsley
1 very finely-chopped onion
2 finely-chopped cloves of garlic
1 tablespoon capers
3–4 tablespoons olive oil
1–1½ tablespoons lemon juice
pepper and salt

Sauces

Pound together the parsley, onions, garlic and capers to mix them well together. Gradually add the oil, mixing all the time, then add the lemon juice and pepper and salt to taste. The sauce should be really thick. It is very good served with hot or cold fish or cold meat.

CAPER SAUCE SALSA DI CAPPERI

1½ oz. butter
1½ oz. flour
1 pint meat stock

2 tablespoons capers
pepper and salt
vinegar if liked

Melt the butter and add the flour; let it brown. Add the hot stock; stir and cook until it thickens. Add the capers, pepper and salt, and a little vinegar if liked. Simmer for 10–15 minutes. Serve with fish.

PRAWN SAUCE SALSA DI GAMBERI

1 medium-sized chopped onion
1 chopped clove of garlic
1 lb. skinned, chopped tomatoes
1 tablespoon olive oil

1 tablespoon butter
chopped parsley
½ lb. shelled cooked prawns
pepper and salt

Brown the onion and garlic in the hot oil and butter. Add the tomatoes, with pepper and salt, simmer for 30 minutes. Add the prawns; cook for 10 minutes, then stir in the chopped parsley and correct the seasoning. Serve with spaghetti or fish.

TOMATO SAUCE (1) SALSA ALLA PIZZAIOLA

1 finely-chopped onion
2 tablespoons olive oil
2 lb. peeled and quartered tomatoes

freshly-ground pepper and salt
1 tablespoon chopped parsley
4 cloves of garlic

Cook the onion and garlic in the hot oil until they soften and colour. Add the tomatoes; squash them with a wooden spoon as

Sauces

they are cooking. Add pepper and salt and cook until the sauce is thick. If you object to the tomato seeds, strain the sauce through a fine sieve. Add the chopped parsley. This sauce can be served with meat, haricot beans or pasta.

TOMATO SAUCE (2) SALSA DI POMIDORO

3 lb. peeled, chopped tomatoes
1 chopped onion
1 chopped clove of garlic
1 finely-chopped celery stalk
pepper and salt
2 teaspoons caster sugar
1 bay leaf
4 chopped fresh basil leaves if available
butter or oil for frying
chopped parsley

Heat the butter or oil in a heavy pan. Add the onion, garlic and celery and cook until the onion softens, then add the tomatoes, salt, pepper, sugar, bay leaf and parsley. Cook gently for about 50–55 minutes. Rub the vegetables through a sieve. Correct the seasoning and add the chopped basil leaves.

TOMATO AND MEAT SAUCE SALSA DI POMIDORO CON CARNE

1 chopped onion
1 chopped carrot
1 chopped clove of garlic
2 oz. chopped mushrooms
2–2½ lb. peeled and quartered tomatoes
4 oz. uncooked minced beef or veal
pepper and salt
1 bay leaf
oil for frying

Fry the onion, carrot, garlic and mushrooms in hot oil until they begin to soften. Add the meat; stir and cook for 3–4 minutes. Add the tomatoes and bay leaf; season to taste. Simmer gently for 50–55 minutes. Pass through a fine sieve, reheat and correct the seasoning.

Sauces

HOT SAUCE LA BAGNA CAUDA

This is a speciality from Piedmont. It is served hot with raw vegetables, such as pimientos, cabbage and cardoons, cut into thin strips. (Cardoons are allied to the globe artichoke. They are cultivated for their stalk, although the heads can be eaten, and have a similar flavour to globe artichokes. They have never been popular in England.)

2 tablespoons oil
2 tablespoons butter
1 tin of anchovy fillets, or 6 salted anchovies
8 finely-chopped cloves of garlic
freshly-ground black pepper

If salted anchovies are used, soak them for 1 hour beforehand. Chop the anchovies and pound them with the garlic. Heat the butter and oil, add the anchovies, garlic and pepper, cook gently for 15 minutes or so. Serve hot.

SWEET-SOUR SAUCE SALSA AGRO-DOLCE

These sweet-sour sauces are typical of Italian cooking. There are many different versions as they are composed to suit the food they are served with. (See Rabbit with Sweet-Sour Sauce, page 128.) Sometimes candied peel and nuts are added. The liquid basis can be water, wine or stock.

1½ oz. butter
1½ oz. flour
1 large chopped onion
2 tablespoons sugar
freshly-ground black pepper
salt
2 tablespoons wine vinegar
1 pint hot stock or water

Heat the butter, add the onion and cook until it softens and colours. Add the flour; stir and let it brown; do not let it burn as this spoils the taste of the sauce. Add the stock or water, vinegar, sugar, pepper and salt. Stir and cook until the sauce is smooth. It is good served with meat balls (see page 103) or meat.

Sauces

SWEET-SOUR SAUCE WITH NUTS SALSA AGRO-DOLCE CON NOCI

- 2 tablespoons wine vinegar
- ½ pint meat stock
- 2 tablespoons sugar
- ¼ lb. finely-chopped pine nuts
- 1 dessertspoon finely-chopped candied peel
- 1 tablespoon sultanas
- 2 tablespoons red currant jelly
- 2–3 small squares of bitter chocolate

Mix all the ingredients together over a low heat until the chocolate has melted. Simmer gently for 20 minutes. Correct the seasoning. Serve with hare, venison or wild boar. Do not be put off by the addition of chocolate; it gives colour and texture. The Spaniards also use it in savoury sauces.

MAYONNAISE MAIONESE

- 3 egg yolks
- about ½ pint best-quality olive oil
- lemon juice
- salt and pepper

Put the egg yolks in a bowl. Add a pinch of salt and pepper. Stir the eggs to break them up. Gradually add the oil, drop by drop at first. Stir all the time; when it emulsifies, the oil can be added more quickly. Continue to add the oil, stirring all the time, until the mayonnaise is thick and smooth. Add a little lemon juice to taste. Correct the seasoning.

TUNA FISH MAYONNAISE MAIONESE TONNATO

Make a mayonnaise as in the preceding recipe. Pound the contents of a small tin of tuna fish until they are smooth. Add slowly to the mayonnaise. Serve with cold meat and fish.

PESTO IL PESTO

This is one of my favourite dressings or sauces. It really must have the fragrance of fresh basil, and there is no substitute. I find

Sauces

that basil grows quite well in pots on a sunny window sill. One can use dried basil, which should be soaked for 15 minutes in a little milk, and marjoram too can be used; but of course these bear no resemblance to fresh basil. Pesto is a typical Genoese sauce. It is also popular in Corsica and in Southern France, where it is added to a soup of beans and potatoes to make their 'Soupe au Pistou'.

2 *good handfuls of finely-chopped basil leaves*	1 *oz. grated Sardo or Parmesan cheese*
3 *or more chopped cloves of garlic*	*pepper and salt*
1 *oz. pine nuts*	2–3 *tablespoons olive oil*

Pound the basil, garlic, pine nuts and olive oil in a mortar. Add the grated cheese, pepper and salt to taste and more olive oil to make a thick creamy mass. Serve with pasta, gnocchi and soups.

FRUIT MUSTARD MOSTARDA DI FRUTTA

This is a most attractive fruit mustard. Mixed fruits, such as pears, half peaches with the stones, tiny oranges, cherries, apricots, plums and melon, are cooked in a sugar syrup and flavoured with garlic and mustard oil. The garlic is not at all obtrusive. This mustard can be bought easily in England and although fairly expensive (about 10s. for a small jar), it is quite unique and goes well with cold meats, especially ham, also poultry and eels.

Desserts

IL DOLCI

Baked Apples in Wine	*Mele in Vino*
Apricots Stuffed with Almond Paste	*Albicocche Marzapane*
Fritters	*Fritelle*
Nut Pudding	*Torta di Noci*
Marsala Egg Fluff	*Zabaglione, Zabaione*
Zabaglione Sauce	*Salsa di Zabaglione*
Macaroons	*Amaretti*
Cheesecake	*Torta di Ricotta*
Mont Blanc	*Monte Bianco*
Peaches in White Wine	*Pesche in Vino Bianco*
Short-Crust Pastry	*Pasta Frolla*
Pastrycook's Custard	*Crema Pasticciera*
Pastrycook's Chocolate Custard	*Crema Pasticciera al Cioccolato*
Pears Regina Margherita	*Pere alla Regina Margherita*
Strawberries in Marsala	*Fragole in Marsala*
Fruit Salad	*Insalata di Frutta*
Stuffed Peaches	*Pesche Ripiene*
Peaches with Zabaglione Sauce	*Pesche con Salsa di Zabaglione*
Sponge Cake	*Pan di Spagna*
Siena Cake	*Panforte di Siena*
Sweet Ravioli	*Ravioli Dolci*
Ricotta Pudding	*Budino di Ricotta*
Cream Cheese with Dried Fruit	*Ricotta con Frutta Secca*
Ice Cream with Candied Fruit and Nuts	*Cassata*

Desserts

Sorbets or Water Ices	*Granite*
Coffee Ice	*Granita al Caffè*
Lemon Ice	*Granita di Limone*
Spumoni	*Spumoni*
Strawberry Spumoni	*Spumoni di Fragole*
Almond Ice	*Gelato di Mandorle*
Italian Nougat	*Torrone*
Cremona Nougat	*Torrone di Cremona*
Chocolate Nougat	*Torrone di Cioccolato*
Italian Trifle	*Zuppa Inglese*

Desserts
IL DOLCI

※※※※※※

In Italy fewer and fewer restaurants serve sweets now. As in France, meals frequently end with cheese or fresh fruit or both. In the past, most trattorias and tavernas served typical sweets but now, if you want to sample the Italians' famous zabaglione or their cakes, you may have to go to a café and eat standing at the bar. This is a pity because they make unusually good 'dolci'.

In Europe the Italians were the pioneers of ice cream and emigrant evangelists were crying 'Hokey Pokey, penny a lump', long before we had learnt what a money spinner 'frozen custards' could be. The Italians have kept their lead in this field with their light fluffy spumoni, creamy gelati, delicious graniti (full-flavoured water ices) and complex compositions such as Sicilian cassata.

The cakes in the pastry shops look rococo—gaudy and over-decorated; rather off-putting, with billiard-green angelica and buxom scarlet cherries. Actually they taste very good.

Cheese and fruit are sometimes eaten together. Bel Paese teams with pears and Gorgonzola with apples. Sometimes fennel is eaten at the end of a meal; it is served with oil and lemon juice and eaten like asparagus with the fingers; its faintly aniseed flavour is most refreshing.

BAKED APPLES IN WINE MELE IN VINO

4 large cooking-apples
2–3 oz. seedless raisins soaked in a wineglass of red wine for 30 minutes

grated rind of 1 orange
3 tablespoons sugar
butter

Desserts

Wipe and core the apples. Fill the cavities with the raisins, orange rind and sugar mixed together. Put the apples in a fireproof dish and top each one with a small piece of butter. Pour in the wine left over from the raisins. Bake for 40–45 minutes in a moderate oven (375°F). Serve hot or cold.

APRICOTS STUFFED WITH ALMOND PASTE
ALBICOCCHE MARZAPANE

1 lb. dried apricots
8 oz. ground almonds
8 oz. icing sugar
1 stiffly-beaten egg white

2–3 drops of almond essence, if a stronger flavour is liked

Soak the apricots in hot water overnight. The next day cook them very gently in the water they were soaked in. Do not let them break up. Mix together the ground almonds, icing sugar and almond essence. Add the egg white, mixing in well. If the paste is too stiff, add a little lemon juice. Fill each apricot with almond paste. Roll them in caster sugar. Leave them to dry in a cool place overnight.

FRITTERS FRITELLE

½ lb. flour
¼ teaspoon salt
3 egg yolks
grated rind of 1 lemon

cold water
oil for deep frying
caster sugar

Sift the flour and salt into a large basin. Put the egg yolks in the centre and gradually work the flour into the eggs. When they are incorporated, slowly add enough cold water to make a light batter, the consistency of double cream. Add the lemon rind; beat well in. Leave for 1 hour. Heat the oil until it is very hot; drop in teaspoons of batter, a few at a time, and fry until golden and light. Drain well. Serve sprinkled with caster sugar.

Desserts

NUT PUDDING TORTA DI NOCI

½ lb. pounded walnuts
½ lb. caster sugar
½ lb. grated bitter chocolate
2 oz. finely-chopped candied peel
5 eggs
1 tablespoon Marsala

Separate the eggs. Add the yolks to the walnuts, sugar, chocolate and peel. Mix well together and add the Marsala. Beat the egg whites stiffly, then fold them in. Butter a fireproof dish, pour in the mixture, bake in a moderate oven (350°F–375°F) for 30 minutes. Serve hot or cold.

MARSALA EGG FLUFF ZABAGLIONE, ZABAIONE

If you order zabaglione in a café-bar you may be given a glass of bottled Marsala-flavoured egg nog, rather like the Dutch Advocaat.

Allow 1½ egg yolks per person.

6 egg yolks
6 tablespoons icing sugar
6 tablespoons Marsala, Madeira or a sweet sherry

Beat the egg yolks and sugar together until they are really light and frothy, then add the wine gradually. Put the mixture in a double boiler over very hot, but not boiling, water. Failing this, put it in a saucepan (or a bowl) which can stand in another pan of hot water; keep the heat low. Now beat continuously until the mixture is smooth and frothy and has thickened slightly. Pour it immediately into warmed cups or glasses and eat it with a spoon. It can also be served chilled and eaten with sponge fingers.

ZABAGLIONE SAUCE SALSA DI ZABAGLIONE

4 egg yolks
3 tablespoons caster sugar
1 tablespoon water
4 tablespoons Marsala, Madeira or sherry

Desserts

Put the sugar, egg yolks and water into a bowl. Beat the mixture until it is light. Add the wine and cook over hot water, beating continuously until the mixture thickens. Serve hot or cold with fruit, or sponge cakes.

MACAROONS AMARETTI

6 oz. ground almonds
2 oz. finely-ground bitter
   almonds

6 oz. caster sugar
2 egg whites
small circles of rice paper

Mix the two kinds of ground almonds together. By using bitter almonds you will get a stronger almond flavour, and it is much better than adding almond essence. Mix in the sugar, then gradually add the egg whites. The mixture should be soft but not liquid. Put the teaspoonfuls of the mixture on the rice paper, already placed on a baking-tray. Cook in a moderate oven (350°F) until they are light brown (about 6–10 minutes). Store in an airtight tin.

CHEESECAKE TORTA DI RICOTTA

½ lb. shortcrust pastry (pasta
   frolla, see page 162)
½ lb. ricotta or other curd cheese
3 tablespoons sugar
½ pint milk

1 egg yolk
3 oz. flour
1 teaspoon grated lemon rind
1 oz. sultanas

Beat the ricotta and sugar together until smooth, add the sultanas and lemon rind. Mix the flour, egg yolk and milk together; cook over a low heat, stirring continuously until the mixture thickens and is creamy, then mix in the ricotta. Roll out the pastry thinly to line a round 7-inch tin or square 6-inch tin. Fill with the cheese mixture which should be at least 1 inch thick. Bake in a moderate oven (350°F) for 30–40 minutes. It should be firm and the top golden-brown. Test with a toothpick.

Desserts

MONT BLANC MONTE BIANCO

Ideally one peels the chestnuts and makes the purée oneself. Purists may shake their heads, but I think one can cheat and use tinned, sweetened French chestnut purée. It has a much better flavour and texture than a purée made from the rather dry chestnuts usually on sale in England.

1 large tin sweetened chestnut purée (1 lb.)
5 fluid oz. double cream

Put the chestnut purée in a fairly large bowl and beat it thoroughly until light. Arrange mounds of it in individual dishes. Whip the cream stiffly and pile it on top. Serve chilled.

PEACHES IN WHITE WINE PESCHE IN VINO BIANCO

Choose large, firm-fleshed yellow peaches for this dish.

4–6 peaches
caster sugar
chilled Asti Spumante or sweet white wine, to cover

Peel the peaches, cut them in half, remove the stones, then slice the peaches finely. Put them in shallow champagne glasses, sprinkle lightly with sugar, chill and, just before serving, pour the chilled wine over.

SHORT-CRUST PASTRY PASTA FROLLA

8 oz. plain flour
3 oz. caster sugar
4 oz. soft, but not melted, butter
½ teaspoon grated lemon rind
2 egg yolks
a small pinch of salt

Sift together the flour, sugar and salt. Make a well in the centre and put in the butter, eggs and lemon rind. Gradually mix in the flour until the dough is smooth. It should not be necessary to add water. Form into a ball, cover with greaseproof paper or aluminium foil and chill for at least 30 minutes. Use as required.

Desserts

PASTRYCOOK'S CUSTARD CREMA PASTICCIERA

½ pint milk
1 oz. flour
3 egg yolks

1 oz. caster sugar
grated rind of 1 small lemon
½ teaspoon vanilla essence

Scald the milk. Put the flour, egg yolks, sugar, lemon rind and vanilla essence into a basin. Beat well together until light. Add the milk slowly, beating all the time. Pour the mixture into a saucepan and cook over a low heat, stirring continuously, until it thickens. To test if it is thick enough, remove the spoon from the custard and make a line down the back of the spoon with the finger; if it does not close up, the custard has cooked enough. Leave it to cool, stirring from time to time to prevent a skin forming. The custard can now be flavoured with Marsala, sherry, brandy, rum or a liqueur.

PASTRYCOOK'S CHOCOLATE CUSTARD CREMA PASTICCIERA AL CIOCCOLATO

½ pint milk
1 oz. flour
3 egg yolks

1 oz. caster sugar
4 oz. plain chocolate (Chocolat Menier is good)

Make the custard as in the preceding recipe. When it is cooked, grate in the chocolate, then stir and cook until the chocolate has completely melted and the custard is smooth.

PEARS REGINA MARGHERITA PERE ALLA REGINA MARGHERITA

4 large eating-pears
1 small glass of fairly sweet white wine
2 tablespoons caster sugar

water
½ pint pastrycook's custard (see above)

Peel the pears carefully with a potato-peeler. Cut them in half and

Desserts

remove the core carefully without breaking the fruit. Put them in a large shallow saucepan or frying-pan, cover with the wine, sugar, and water, so that the pears are just covered. Simmer very gently until the pears are cooked. Remove and leave to cool; pour the juice round and, when the pears are cold, fill the cavities with the cold custard.

STRAWBERRIES IN MARSALA FRAGOLE IN MARSALA

2–3 small punnets of strawberries *1 gill of Marsala or sherry*
sugar to taste

Clean and hull the strawberries, sprinkle with sugar and pour the wine over. Serve cold.

FRUIT SALAD INSALATA DI FRUTTA

peaches, grapes, apples, pears *1 liqueur glass of Strega*
caster sugar

Peel the fruit and remove stones, cores and pips. Cut it up small. Cover with sugar and Strega (a delicious Italian liqueur). Leave it to macerate for a few hours, then put it in the refrigerator. Serve really cold.

STUFFED PEACHES PESCHE RIPIENE

6 large yellow peaches *3–4 oz. almond macaroons*
1 extra peach for the filling *1 tablespoon unsalted butter*
1–2 tablespoons sugar (or sugar *1 egg yolk*
to taste) *butter for cooking*

Leave the skin on the six peaches, cut them in half and remove the stones and some of the pulp. Put this pulp in a basin. Pound the macaroons finely. Peel the extra peach; this can be done by stroking the skin with the back of a knife, or by putting the peach

Desserts

in hot water for a minute. Add this peach, cut up, to the pulp in the basin, then add the macaroons. Crack the peach stones, peel the kernels and chop them finely; add these, and the sugar and egg yolk, to the pulp. Mix well together. Arrange the peach halves in a buttered fireproof dish, fill each half with the mixture, put a small piece of butter on top. Cook in a moderate oven (350°F–375°F) for 30–35 minutes. Serve hot or cold.

PEACHES WITH ZABAGLIONE SAUCE PESCHE CON SALSA DI ZABAGLIONE

4 firm peaches
1 gill of water
a liqueur glass of Strega, Marsala or rum
2 tablespoons water
½ pint Zabaglione sauce (see page 160)
4 slices of sponge cake

Cut the peaches in half; remove the stones. Mix together the water, sugar and liqueur, pour the mixture over the peaches and leave to macerate for an hour or two. Arrange two peach halves on each piece of sponge cake, pour the juice round and cover with the Zabaglione sauce.

SPONGE CAKE PAN DI SPAGNA

5 egg yolks
6 oz. caster sugar
grated rind of 1 lemon
4 oz. plain sifted flour
1 teaspoon vanilla essence
stiffly-beaten egg whites

Beat the egg yolks and sugar together until lemon coloured. Add the flour, gradually folding it in. Add the lemon rind and vanilla. Fold in the stiffly-beaten egg whites; do this as gently as possible, so as to enclose all the air and not stir it out. Grease and lightly-flour an 8-inch sandwich tin. Put in the mixture and bake in a moderate oven (350°F–375°F) for 35–40 minutes. Do not overcook, or the texture will be spoilt. When the cake is cooked, invert it on a cake rack and leave to cool. Remove it carefully from the tin.

Desserts

SIENA CAKE PANFORTE DI SIENA

3 oz. self-raising flour
4 oz. shelled, blanched, coarsely-chopped and roasted almonds
2 oz. shelled, coarsely-chopped and roasted hazel nuts
4 oz. chopped mixed candied peel
2 oz. unsweetened cocoa
½ teaspoon freshly-ground nutmeg
½ teaspoon powdered cinnamon
3 oz. granulated sugar
4 fluid oz. honey
2 tablespoons icing sugar mixed with
1 tablespoon powdered cinnamon for topping

Mix together the flour, chopped nuts, peel, cocoa, nutmeg and cinnamon. Heat the sugar and honey together in a heavy saucepan, stirring constantly. Cook slowly until a little put in cold water forms a soft ball, or, if you have a sugar thermometer, until 238°F. Remove from the heat, add the nut mixture, stir well together. Line an 8-inch cake tin with greased greaseproof paper and fill with the mixture. Smooth over the top. Bake in a slow oven (300°F) for 30–35 minutes. Let the cake cool, then remove it carefully from the tin. When it is quite cold, sprinkle with the sugar and cinnamon mixture. This cake keeps very well in a cool place.

SWEET RAVIOLI RAVIOLI DOLCI

Ravioli dough (see page 50)
½ *lb. ricotta or other curd cheese*
1 *tablespoon sugar*
1 *oz. finely-chopped candied peel*
1 *beaten egg yolk*
oil for deep frying

Divide the dough in two and roll out each piece very thinly. Mix together the cheese, sugar, candied peel and egg yolk; the mixture should be smooth and light. Cut the dough into circles about 3 inches in diameter, put a teaspoonful of the cheese mixture on each piece, fold in half, seal well with a little water and pinch the edges together. The ravioli should look like miniature Cornish pasties. Let the oil get hot, but not smoking, and fry a few ravioli at a time, until they are golden-brown. Drain well. Keep them hot while cooking the rest. Serve hot, sprinkled with caster sugar.

Desserts

RICOTTA PUDDING BUDINO DI RICOTTA

8 oz. ricotta or other curd cheese	2 oz. ground almonds
2 eggs	1 tablespoon sultanas
3 oz. caster sugar	grated rind of 1 lemon

Separate the eggs. Beat the cheese until it is smooth, then add the egg yolks, ground almonds, sugar and lemon rind. Beat well together until the mixture is well mixed and smooth. Fold in the stiffly-beaten egg whites. Lightly butter a 6–7-inch tin, preferably one with a loose bottom. Pour in the mixture and cook in a moderate oven (350°F–370°F) for 40–45 minutes. It should be firm when cooked. A toothpick inserted should come out quite clean. Leave for 10 minutes before removing from the tin. Serve tepid or cold, sprinkled with caster sugar.

CREAM CHEESE WITH DRIED FRUIT RICOTTA CON FRUTTA SECCA

½ lb. ricotta or other curd cheese	1 tablespoon finely-chopped candied peel
1 oz. finely-chopped blanched almonds	1 tablespoon chopped glacé cherries
1 tablespoon seedless raisins	1 beaten egg yolk
1 tablespoon sultanas	

Mix all the ingredients together. Serve chilled with caster sugar.

ICE CREAM WITH CANDIED FRUIT AND NUTS CASSATA

Cassata can be an ice cream, or a rich cream cake made with ricotta.

1 pint milk	2 oz. finely-chopped candied fruits, such as cherries, angelica, and lemon or orange peel
¼ lb. sugar	
4 egg yolks	
2 tablespoons Marsala	
1 oz. grilled chopped hazel nuts	

Desserts

Put the sugar and egg yolks in a double saucepan and cook and stir until they thicken. Gradually add the boiling milk and the Marsala. Cook slowly, stirring all the time, but do not let the mixture boil. When it has thickened, let it cool; stir now and again to prevent a skin from forming. Stir in the chopped candied fruits and hazel nuts. Freeze in the ice trays at the lowest temperature. After 30 minutes put the mixture in an iced bowl and beat well. Return the mixture to the freezing-trays and leave for 2½–3 hours.

SORBETS OR WATER ICES GRANITE

One of the best coffee water ices I have ever had was in Naples on a very hot and sticky evening. I shall always remember how refreshing and stimulating it was.

COFFEE ICE GRANITA AL CAFFÈ

5 oz. finely-ground Continental roast coffee
4 oz. caster sugar
1½ pints boiling water

Put the coffee in a heavy pan, pour the boiling water on it, then add the sugar and stir until it dissolves. Simmer on a low heat for 15–20 minutes. Strain, let it cool, then pour it into the freezing-trays of your refrigerator. Freeze at the usual ice-making temperature for about 3 hours. There is no need to stir it, as it is meant to be grainy or granulated.

LEMON ICE GRANITA DI LIMONE

½ pint fresh lemon juice (6–8 lemons, depending on their juiciness)
6 oz. sugar
1 pint water
thinly-pared rind of 2 lemons

Put all the ingredients into a saucepan. Bring to the boil and simmer gently for 3–4 minutes. Allow to cool, then remove the lemon peel. Pour the mixture into the freezing-trays. Freeze for about 3 hours at the normal ice-freezing temperature.

Desserts

Orange ice is made in the same way as the lemon ice; but if the oranges are sweet, 4 oz. sugar should be sufficient.

SPUMONI

Spuma is usually just a fruit whip, but spumoni ('big foam') are rich ices made with cream; they can be flavoured with vanilla and have nuts and chopped crystallized fruits mixed in. They can also be made with soft fruit, such as strawberries or raspberries.

STRAWBERRY SPUMONI SPUMONI DI FRAGOLE

2 lb. cleaned and hulled strawberries
3 tablespoons caster sugar (or sugar to taste)
juice of 1 lemon
1 pint double cream
3 oz. icing sugar

Put the strawberries through a sieve. Add the lemon juice and sugar and mix in well. Whip the cream until stiff and fold in the icing sugar, then add it to the strawberry purée. Put the mixture into a mould and chill.

ALMOND ICE GELATO DI MANDORLE

¾ pint milk
4 oz. caster sugar
4 oz. ground almonds
5 fluid oz. cream
1 level teaspoon gelatine
1 separated egg
a few drops of almond essence to taste
6 blanched, chopped and roasted almonds

Soften the gelatine in a little cold water, add it to the warm milk and cook gently until the gelatine has dissolved. Add the sugar; stir it in. Add the slightly-beaten egg yolk; cook for 1-2 minutes, stirring all the time. Leave to cool, then beat thoroughly. Fold in the stiffly-beaten egg white and the whipped cream. Stir in the ground almonds and add the almond essence. Freeze. Serve sprinkled with the chopped almonds.

Desserts

ITALIAN NOUGAT TORRONE

The Italians make wonderful nougat (torrone), both hard and soft. As the French have their delicately coloured sugared almonds (dragées) for special occasions—christenings, weddings and First Communions—so the Italians have their torrones on feast days. Their famous Panforte di Siena (see page 166), made with almonds, candied fruits, spices, flour, butter and eggs—a cross between nougat and fruit cake—is exported all over the world. Torrone di Cremona (see below) is a hard nougat made with egg whites, honey, sugar, roasted almonds and candied peel. There are also chocolate torrones, and many other flavours.

CREMONA NOUGAT TORRONE DI CREMONA

1 lb. blanched, skinned and roasted almonds
½ lb. granulated sugar
4 fluid oz. thin honey
2 stiffly-beaten egg whites
1 teaspoon finely-chopped candied peel
½ teaspoon cinnamon

Chop the almonds and pound them in a mortar with the sugar, then add the candied peel and cinnamon. Put the honey in a heavy pan, add the almond mixture and stir and cook until the mixture begins to brown. Remove from the heat and quickly fold in the egg whites. Use a shallow tin, approximately 10 by 8 inches and at least 2½ inches deep; line it with rice paper; pour in the mixture; let it cool, then cut it into small rectangular pieces.

CHOCOLATE NOUGAT TORRONE DI CIOCCOLATO

4 fluid oz. honey
½ lb. granulated sugar
6 oz. cocoa blended with 2 tablespoons water
2 stiffly-beaten egg whites
1 lb. shelled, finely-chopped and roasted hazel nuts

Heat the honey and sugar together in a heavy saucepan until they begin to brown. Add the beaten egg whites gradually; mix them in well. Cook the cocoa with the water until smooth, stirring all

Desserts

the time; then add it, and the nuts, to the honey mixture. Line a shallow tin with rice paper and pour in the mixture; the tin should be approximately 10 by 8 inches; the mixture should be about 2 inches deep. Let it cool, then cut it into small rectangles.

ITALIAN TRIFLE ZUPPA INGLESE

Zuppa Inglese is an odd title for a showy sweet. It means literally English soup and no one seems to know how it got its name. Like sherry trifle, it has endless varieties.

3 8-*inch sponge cakes (see page 165)*	4 *oz. caster sugar*
	Marsala
1 *pint pastrycook's custard (see page 163)*	*chopped glacé cherries and strips of angelica*
4 *very stiffly-beaten egg whites*	

Cut the sponge cakes in halves. Put one half on a lightly greased baking-tray. Sprinkle well with Marsala; let this soak in. Put a thin layer of custard on top, then another half sponge cake. Continue in this way, ending with a half sponge cake. Use plenty of Marsala. Fold the sugar into the egg whites; beat for 2–3 minutes. Cover the cake completely with the meringue; rough it up. Put the cake in a slow oven (280°F) until the meringue is lightly coloured and crisp (about 20–30 minutes). Decorate with cherries and angelica.

Cheeses
I FORMAGGI

Some of the best cheeses in the world come from Italy and many of them can be bought in this country.

BEL PAESE
A soft, mild cheese made from cow's milk. Often used in cooking as it melts at a low temperature. It can be used as a substitute for Mozzarella.

FIOR DI LATTE
A rather tasteless cheese; a little like a Mozzarella, but made from cow's milk instead of buffalo's milk.

FONTINA
This is a very rich, full fat, creamy cheese. It is made in Piedmont and is used for their famous fonduta.

GORGONZOLA
Comes from Lombardy. It is made from cow's milk and is a creamy blue-veined cheese, one of the best of its type.

MASCARPONE OR MARSCHEPONE
Rather like the French 'fromage blanc' or 'petit Suisse'. It is usually sold wrapped in butter muslin. It is made from fresh cream and is soft textured. Candied fruit can be added, or it can be flavoured with coffee, or beaten with brandy and sprinkled with fine sugar.

MOZZARELLA
This should be made from buffalo's milk, but now is very often

Cheeses

made from cow's milk as the buffalo is being used less and less. It can be used for cooking as it melts easily.

PARMESAN or PARMIGIANO
This unique cheese is made from skimmed milk. It is ideal for cooked dishes as it is easily grated and never becomes tacky. It is possible to buy matured Parmesan in Soho; and the more mature it is, the better it tastes. A young, soft Parmesan is quite delicious eaten with a crusty loaf, in the same way as Cheddar or any other hard cheese.

PECORINO
This is a general term for hard, sharp cheese. It is usually made from ewe's milk. Can be used instead of Parmesan.

PROVOLA
Ideally this should be made from buffalo's milk. It is sometimes smoked.

PROVOLONE
Made from buffalo's or cow's milk. It comes in various shapes and sizes; round, large sausage-shape, pear-shape and cylindrical. It is rather tasteless.

RICOTTA
This is a soft curd cheese made from ewe's milk. It can be eaten as it is, with sugar, or used in cooking for cheesecakes, gnocchi and as a filling for ravioli.

SARDO
This is made in Sardinia. It is a sharp pecorino-type cheese.

STRACCHINO
A soft, creamy cheese. A really good one has an incomparable flavour.

Drinks and Aperitifs
BEVANDE E APERITIVI

Many of the best and most interesting aperitifs come from Italy and quite a few are obtainable in England. The best known are the vermouths: Martini, Martini Rossi (red), Martini Bianchi (white), Gancia, Cinzano (white or red), Cinzano Amaro (bitter) and Carpano Punt y Mes. They can be sweet or dry, and vary from almost colourless to dark brown. They are made by macerating various herbs in strong wine.

In Italy, I have drunk some strange aperitifs. Cynar, made from globe artichokes is pleasantly bitter and supposed to be good for the liver. Rabarbaro, made from rhubarb, is slightly sweeter. I also had a eucalyptus-flavoured one made by the Trappist monks at Tre Fontana near Rome (it was here that the head of St. Paul was supposed to have bounced three times and in each place where the head touched a fountain sprung up). I did not like it at all, although it may taste better than some cough mixtures.

Campari is clean-flavoured and refreshingly bitter. In Italy it is often sold in small crown-capped bottles when one asks for a Campari Soda. There is also a white Campari liqueur.

Fernet Branca is made from a great many herbs. It is a good pick-me-up for a hangover. To cut its excessive bitterness, try it with a little crème de menthe or crème de Cassis (blackcurrant liqueur).

Wines
VINI

ASTI SPUMANTE
Light, sparkling sweet white wine from Piedmont.

Drinks

BAROLO
Red wine, rather heady. Famous for centuries.

BARBERA
Dry or sweet, red or white from Piedmont.

CHIANTI
A Tuscany wine exported to England for over 300 years. The bottles are straw covered.

EST! EST! EST!
White wine, sweet or dry. Famous for centuries.

FALERNO
One of the oldest known wines, from Campania.

FRASCATI
Tingling, dry white wine. One of the 'vini dei castelli' from the Alban Hills near Rome.

LACRIMA CHRISTI
From Campania, red or white. Rather like a Rhine wine.

MOSCATO
A white fortified wine, heavy and very sweet.

ORVIETO
White wine, dry or sweet, from Umbria. Rather like a Sauterne.

SOAVE
Excellent white wine, rather like Chablis, from the Veneto.

VALPOLICELLA
Red, rather sweet wine, from the Veneto.

Liqueurs and Spirits
LIQUORI E ACQUAVATI

MARSALA
Popular in England since the eighteenth century. Like sherry it is a fortified wine. Very useful in cooking, for both sweet and savoury dishes.

MARASCHINO
Made from bitter cherries. Famous all over the world.

MILLEFIORE
Very sweet, with a twig in the bottle on which the sugar crystallizes.

MORETTA
Coffee-flavoured.

RATAFIA
Made from black cherry kernels or almonds

AURUM
Has a pleasant orange flavour.

STREGA
Rather like a Chartreuse. Flavoured with herbs and spices.

BRANDA
Italian brandies cannot be compared to the French. Stock is probably the best.

GRAPPA
Like a French marc, made from a distillation of the grape pressings.

Index

NOTE: *There is a list of recipes at the beginning of each section in English and Italian. The Italian name is only shown in the index when it is in common use or when there is no adequate English translation.*

Agnolotti, 49
Alfabeto, 48
Almond Ice, 169
Almond Paste, 159
Almond Sauce, 149
Amaretti, 161
Anchovies with Pimientos, 34
Anchovy and Cheese Sandwiches, 29
Anchovy Sauce, 64, 130
Antipasti, 25
Apples with Wine, 158
Apricots Stuffed with Almond Paste, 159
Artichokes:
  Baked, 137
  Hearts in Olive Oil, 28
  Jewish Style, 136
Asparagus:
  with Parmesan, 137
  Wild, 137
Asti Spumante, 116, 174
Aubergine:
  Baked, 138
  Fried, 138
  in Tomato Sauce, 29

Barbera, 175
Barolo, 175
Basil, 19

Basil, Pesto, 16, 39, 154
Bay Leaf, 19
Beans:
  French, 139
  French, Salad, 29
Beef:
  Broth, 38
  Stew, Bolognese, 104
  Stew, with Cloves, 103
Bel Paese, 172
Blackbirds and Thrushes, 18
Boar, Wild, 100
Bocconcini, 119
Boiled Dinner, Italian (Bollito), 101
Brains, 111
Branda, 176
Broccoli, 138
Broth:
  Beef, 38
  Chicken, 38
Bucatini, 48
Buttàriga (Grey Mullet Roe), 26

Cabbage, Sharp, 139
Cakes:
  Cheese, 161
  Siena, 166
  Sponge, 165
Calabrian Sauce, 150

Index

Calamari (Squid), 91
Calf's Liver, 110, 112
Calf's Tongues, 109
Campari, 174
Cannelloni, 48, 49, 59
Capeletti, 49
Capelli d'Angelo, 48
Capellini, 48
Caper Sauce, 151
Cappon Magro, 16, 89
Cardoons, 153
Carpano Punt y Mes, 174
Carrots with Marsala, 142
Cassata, 167
Cauliflower:
  Fried, 112
  Soufflé, 139
Cheese and Anchovy Sandwiches, 29
Cheeses, 172, 173
Cheesecake, 161
Cheese, Cream with Dried Fruit, 167
Chestnuts, 13
  Monte Bianco, 162
  Purée, 141
  Soup, 41
  Stewed, 141
Chianti, 175
Chick Peas, 141
Chicken:
  Breasts Lombardy Style, 122
  Breasts Valdostana, 123
  Broth, 38
  Diavolo, 123
  Hunter Style, 124
  with Olives, 124
  with Pimientos, 125
  with Rice Salad, 125
  Stuffed with Pine Nuts, 124
  in Tuna Fish Sauce, 125
Chicken Livers:
  with Eggs, 82
  with Noodles, 53
  with Noodles, Soup, 43
  with Polenta, 67
  with Rice, 74
Chocolate Custard, Pastrycook's, 163
Chocolate Torrone, 170
Cinnamon, 22
Cinzano, Bitter, Red, White, 174
Cloves, 22
Cloves, Beef Stew, 103
Cod, Salt, Vicenza, 97
Coffee Ice, 168
Conchiglie, 49
Consommé with Pesto, 39
Coppa, 27
Corn Meal (Polenta), 65
  Baked, 66
  Boiled, 66
  with Chicken Livers, 67
  Dumplings, 67
Cotechino, 27, 101
Courgettes:
  Fried, 140
  Stewed, 140
  Stuffed, 140
Couscous, Sicilian, 88
Crawfish Fra Diavolo, 87
Cream Sauce, 132
Crostini, 26
Cucumber Salad, 30
Custard, Chocolate, Pastrycook's, 163
Custard, Pastrycook's, 163
Cuttlefish, 91

Desserts, 156–71
Ditali, 48
Dough, Pasta, 50
Duck, with Macaroni, 126
Duck, Roast with Olives, 126
Dumplings:
  Baked, 62
  Bolognese Style, Soup, 64
  Potato, 63

Index

Potato, Green, 63
Romagna, Spinach, in Broth, 64
Semolina, 63
Semolina, Saffron, 65

Eels, 91
Eggs:
  with Chicken Livers, 82
  Florentine, 82
  Hard-boiled with Curd Cheese, 83
  with Lentil Purée, 81
  with Parmesan Cheese, 81
  Ragged, Soup, 39
  Rossini, 81
  with Tuna Fish Mayonnaise, 31
  Omelettes, 83
    Pimiento, 84
    Potato, 83
Est! Est! Est! 175
Eucalyptus Liqueur, 174

Falerno, 175
Farfalle, 49
Farfalline, 49
Farsumagru, 119
Fennel, 19, 32, 158
Fernet Branca, 174
Fettuccine, 48
Fideline, 48
Figs with Raw Ham, 35
Fior di Latte, 172
Fish:
  Crawfish Fra Diavolo, 87
  Eels, Stewed, 91
  Lake Trout, 91
  Mixed, Fried, 93
  Mussels, Oven-baked, 94
  Octopus, Squid, Cuttlefish, 91
  Poached, 93
  Prawn and Raw Mushroom Salad, 31
  Prawns, Fried, 93
  Prawns with Ham, 94
  Red Mullet, Cooked in Paper Cases, 95
  Red Mullet, Leghorn Style, 95
  Roast, 92
  Salad, 30, 89
  Salt Cod, Vicenza, 97
  Scampi, Fried, 93
  Sea Bass, 95
  Sicilian Couscous, 88
  Skate, Baked, 96
  Soles, Venetian Style, 96
  Soup, Rimini, 44
  Squid, Neapolitan Style, 92
  Stew Genoese, 44
  Tuna Fish with Haricot Beans, 30
    Fresh, Bologna Style, 91
    Mayonnaise with Eggs, 31
    Tomatoes stuffed with, 32
    and Potato Salad, 33
Fontina, 172
Fritters, 159
Fritto Misto, 93, 111
Fruit:
  Candied with Guinea Fowl, 127
  Dried with Ricotta, 167
  Mustard, 155
  Salad, 164
Fry, Mixed, 111
Fry, Mixed, Fish, 93
Fry, Mixed, on Skewers, 113
Fungi, Edible, 12–13

Game, 121–32
Gancia, 174
Garlic, 20
Ginger, 22
Gnocchi:
  Baked, 62
  Potato, 63
  Potato, Green, 63
  Semolina, 63
Goat, 100
Gorgonzola, 172

Index

Goulash, 104
Grappa, 176
Green Sauce, 150

Ham:
  with Peas, 143
  with Prawns, 94
  Raw, 16, 27
  Raw with Figs, 35
  Raw with Melon, 35

Ice:
  Almond, 169
  with Candied Fruit and Nuts, 167
  Coffee, 168
  Lemon, 168
  Orange, 169
  Spumoni, 169
  Strawberry, 169
Italian Boiled Dinner (Bollito), 101
Italian Dressing, 33

Juniper, 20

Kid, 100
Kid, Roast, 128
Kidneys with Marsala, 111
Kidneys Stewed with White Wine, 110

Lacrima Christi, 175
Lamb:
  Chops, Milan Style, 105
  Roast, 105
  Roast, Baby, 106
  Stewed, 105
  Offal, Stewed, 106
  Tongues with Orange, 107
  Types of, 100
Lasagne, 48
Lasagne Green, Baked, 56
Lasagne Green, to Make, 50

Lemon Ice, 168
Linguine, 48
Liqueurs, 176
Liver, Calf's, 112
Liver, Calf's with Parmesan, 110
Lobster, Spiny, 87

Macaroni:
  Baked, 57
  with Duck, 126
  with Ricotta, 56
Macaroons, 161
Mace, 22
Maraschino, 176
Marjoram, Sweet, 20
Marjoram, Wild, 20
Marsala, 176
Marsala with Carrots, 142
Marsala, Strawberries in, 164
Marsala Egg Fluff, 160
Martini, Red and White, 174
Mascarpone, 172
Mascherpone, 172
Mayonnaise, 154
Mayonnaise, Tuna Fish, 154
Meat, 98–120
Meat Balls, 103
Meat and Tomato Sauce, 152
Melon and Raw Ham, 35
Millefiore, 176
Minestrone:
  Florentine, 40
  Genoese, 42
  Milan, 42
Mint, 20
Monte Bianco, 162
Moretta, 176
Mortadella, 27
Moscato, 175
Mozzarella, 12, 172
Mullet, Grey, Roe, 26
Mullet, Red, Leghorn, 95
Mullet, Red, in Paper, 95

Index

Mushrooms:
  Raw, and Prawn Salad, 31
  Stuffed, 143
  Trifolati, 143
Mussels:
  Oven-Baked, 94
  Pizza, 77
  with Risotto, 71
  with Vermicelli, 55
Mustard, Fruit, 155

Noodles:
  with Basil, 52
  with Chicken Livers, 53
  with Hare Sauce, 57
  Soup with Chicken Livers, 43
Nougat:
  Chocolate, 170
  Cremona, 170
  Italian, 170
Nut Pudding, 160
Nuts with Sweet-Sour Sauce, 154
Nutmeg, 22

Octopus, 91
Olives, Fried, Stuffed, 35
Olives with Chicken, 124
Olive Oil, 12
Omelettes, 83
Omelettes, Pimiento, 84
Omelette, Potato, 83
Onions, Stuffed, 142
Orange Ice, 169
Oregano, 20
Orvietto, 175
Osso Bucco, 118

Pancetta, 27
Panforte, Siena, 166
Parmesan Cheese, 12, 173
Parsley, 20
Partridges, Milan Style, 129

Pasta:
  Basic Dough, 50
  To Cook, 49
  Types of, 48
Pastella (Frying Batter), 112
Pasties, Florentine, 146
Pastry, Short-crust, 162
Pastrycook's Chocolate Custard, 163
Pastrycook's Custard, 163
Peaches, Stuffed, 164
Peaches in White Wine, 162
Peaches with Zabaglione, 165
Pears Regina Margherita, 163
Peas with Raw Ham, 143
Pecorino, 173
Pesto, 16, 154
  wtih Consommé, 39
  with Noodles, 52
Pimiento Omelette, 84
  Salad, 34
Pimientos with Anchovies, 34
  and Tomatoes, 144
Pine Nuts, 12, 124
Pizza:
  Dough, Basic, 76
  Four Seasons, 77
  Franciscan, 78
  with Mussels, 77
  Neapolitan, 78
  Rustic, 78
Polenta:
  Baked, 66
  Boiled, 66
  with Chicken Livers, 67
  Dumplings, 67
Polpette, 72, 73
Pork:
  Chops with Fennel, 108
  with Orange, 107
  Products, 27
  Roast, Florentine, 109
  Roast, Perugian, 109

Index

Pork—*cont.*
  Shoulder, Cured, 27
  Types of, 100
Potato:
  Croquettes, 144
  Fried with Rosemary, 145
  with Milk, 144
  Omelette, 83
  Salad, 32, 33
  Salad and Tuna Fish, 33
Poultry, 121–32
Prawn Sauce, 151
Prawns, Fried, 93
Prawns with Ham, 94
Prawns with Raw Mushroom Salad, 31
Prosciutto, 27
Pudding, Nut, 160
Pudding, Ricotta, 167

Rabarbaro, 174
Rabbit, Hunter Style, 129
Rabbit, Sweet-Sour Sauce, 128
Ratafia, 176
Ravioli, 49
Ravioli, to Make, 50, 58, 166
Ravioli with Cheese Filling, 59
Ravioli with Meat Filling, 59
Ravioli, Sweet, 166
Red Mullet Leghorn Style, 95
Red Mullet Cooked in Paper Cases, 95
Regional Food, 15
Rice, 15, 68–74
  and Aubergines, 70
  Balls, 72
  and Chicken Livers, 74
  and Chicken Salad, 125
  Milanese, 70
  Mould (Sartù), 72
  with Mussels, 71
  and Peas, 41
Ricotta, 12, 173
  Cheesecake, 161
  with Dried Fruit, 167
  with Hard-Boiled Eggs, 83
  with Macaroni, 56
  Stuffed Ravioli, 59
Risi e Bisi, 41
Rissoles (Polpette), 73
Rosemary, 21

Saffron, 21
Sage, 21
Salads:
  Chicken and Rice, 125
  Cucumber, 30
  Fish, 89
  French Bean Salad, 29
  Fruit, 164
  Mixed, 30
  Pimiento, Red, 34
  Potato, 32, 33
  Potato and Tuna Fish, 33
  Prawn and Raw Mushroom, 31
  Tomato, 34
Salad Dressing, Italian, 33
Salami, Genoa, 28
Salami, Milan, 28
Saltimbocca, 118
Sandwiches, Cheese and Anchovy, 29
Sardo, 173
Sartù (Rice Mould), 72
Sauces:
  Almond, 149
  Anchovy, 64, 130
  Brown, 150
  Calabrian, 150
  Caper, 151
  Cream, 132
  Green, 150
  Hare, 57
  Hot (Bagna Cauda), 153
  Meat, 51
    Bolognese, 53
    and Tomato, 152

Index

Piquant, 65
Prawn, 151
Sweet-Sour, 153
Sweet-Sour, with Nuts, 154
Tomato, 73, 151, 152
Tuna Fish, 116
Zabaglione, 116, 160
Scampi, Fried, 93
Sea Bass, 95
Siena Cake, 166
Skate, Baked, 96
Soave, 175
Sole, Venetian Style, 96
Soups:
  Bean, 39
  Beef Broth, 38
  Chestnut, 41
  Chicken Broth, 38
  Chicken Livers with Noodles, 43
  Egg, Ragged, 39
  Fish, Genoese, 44
  Fish Rimini, 44
  Green, 40
  Minestrone, Florentine, 40
    Genoa, 42
    Milan, 42
  Pavia, 39
  Rice and Pea, 41
  Tripe, 43
Spaghetti:
  Bolognese, 53
  with Eggs and Bacon, 51
  with Oil and Garlic, 52
  with Meat Balls, 55
  with Meat Sauce, 51
  with Mushrooms, 54
  Syracuse Style, 54
Spaghettini, 48
Spices, 22, 23
Spinach:
  Croquettes, 145
  with Parmesan, 146
  Pudding, 145
  Roman Style, 146
Spirits, 176
Sponge Cake, 165
Spumoni, 169
Spumoni, Strawberry, 169
Squid, 91
Squid Neapolitan Style, 92
Steak Florentine, 102
Steak with Tomato and Garlic Sauce, 102
Stracchino, 173
Strawberries in Marsala, 164
Strawberry Spumoni, 169
Strega, 164, 176
Sweetbreads, 111

Tagliatelli, 48
Taglierini, 48
Tarragon, 21,
Thrushes, 18
Thyme, 21
Tomato:
  and Meat Sauce, 152
  Salad, 34
  Sauce, 73, 151, 152
  Sauce with Aubergines, 29
  Stuffed with Tuna, 32
Tongues, Calf's, 109
Tongues, Lambs' with Oranges, 107
Torrone, Chocolate, 170
Torrone, Cremona, 170
Tortelline, 49
Trifle, Italian, 171
Tripe, Baked, 113
  Soup, 43
  Stewed, 114
Trout, Lake, 97
Truffles, Black, 17
  White, 15, 123
Tubetti, 48
Tuna Fish:
  Bologna Style, 91
  Eggs, 26

Index

Tuna Fish—*Cont.*
 with Eggs, 31
 with Haricot Beans, 30
 Mayonnaise, 154
 and Potato Salad, 33
Turkey, Boiled, 130
Turnips, Stewed, 147

Valpolicella, 175
Vanilla, 23
Veal:
 Bocconcini, 119
 Chops with Mushrooms, 114
 Cutlets, 114
 Cutlets, Breaded, Milan Style, 115
 Escalopes, 115
 Farsumagru, 119
 Hollow Bone Stew (Osso Bucco), 118
 Mixed Fry, 111
 Rolls, Stuffed, 120
 Saltimbocca, 118
 Stew, 117
 Stew, Sicilian, 117
 Stuffed, Genoese, 119
 with Tuna Fish Sauce, 116
 Types of, 100
 with Zabaglione, 115
Vegetables, 133–47
Venison, Chops with Cream Sauce, 131
Venison, Roast, 131
Vermicelli, 48
Vermicelli with Anchovies, 54
Vermicelli with Mussels, 55
Vermouth, 174

Wine, Apples in, 158
Wines, 13, 174–5

Zabaglione, 160
 Sauce, 160
 Sauce with Veal, 115
Zampone, 28
Ziti, 48
Zuppa Inglese, 171

2200